ISBN

The Chapter in Fiction

The Chapter in Fiction

Theories of
Narrative Division

———◄••••►———

Philip Stevick

SYRACUSE UNIVERSITY PRESS

FOR

Ann

Philip Stevick is professor of English at Temple University, Philadelphia. He is the editor of *The Theory of the Novel* (1967) and *Anti-Story: An Anthology of Experimental Fiction* (1970). His articles have appeared in *Criticism, University of Toronto Quarterly, Western Humanities Review,* and other scholarly journals. He received the B.A. and M.A. degrees from Kent State University and the Ph.D. from Ohio State University.

Contents

Contents

Preface

IT WAS STERNE who first delighted and annoyed me into beginning what has become a book about chapters. I have dealt largely with fiction more conventional than *Tristram Shandy*; yet I have come back several times to *Tristram Shandy* to support points in my argument since Sterne's book, like no other, asks implicitly all those questions which I have tried to lever up and make explicit. Why are novels divided into chapters? What difference does it make that they are? By what devices of craft and by what acts of the imagination are novels so divided? Because of what historical sanctions and esthetic pressures has it seemed necessary, throughout the whole history of fiction, so to divide fiction?

Every book is its own justification, and it is impossible for me to indicate in a prefatory way why I think the questions are important ones—that is what the text that follows should do. Still, I can suggest here what I believe to be true: that the imaginative use of chapters palpably alters the vision and the import of novels, that even the lesser conventions of chapter-making have been the objects of meticulous craftsmanship—even of loving concern—of the greatest of novelists, and that every aspect of the reader's response to fiction, from his most basic appreciation of its techniques to his deepest sensitivity to its meanings, is enhanced by recognition of the chapter as a fact of fiction.

At a few points, by way of discussing historical antecedents or the evidence for assuming the universality of certain structural principles, I have considered works prior to the eighteenth century. The book that follows, all the same, is about the novel, as that genre is ordinarily understood, with *Don Quixote* its great progenitor and its English birth in the masters of the eighteenth century. The examples come largely from fiction in English because that is the fiction which I know best, which I can assume the readers of this book will know best, and because its richness provides abundant instances of those aspects of fictional construction which I wish to discuss, though occasionally I have cited Continental fiction where it has seemed pertinent to some special point. There are few works on fiction that are encyclopedic—Scholes' and Kellogg's *Nature of Narrative* in one sense, Ernest Baker's *History of the English Novel* in another. It has seemed to me no act of cultural myopia to write about the novel largely from the evidence of Anglo-American fiction—a fiction extensive enough to have included most of the options that could have occurred to novelists of other cultures. If my treatment suggests to the reader other possibilities which I have not considered, then so much the better.

I have sought to combine a variety of methods—psychological, formalist, contextualist, and historical—on the assumption that purity of method is not very desirable when dealing with an area that seems not resolvable into a single problem at all but is rather a cluster of related problems. Had I been considering a classic area of fictional theory, widely recognized and frequently discussed, I would have begun historically. Some of my friends have persuaded me, however, without even trying to, that I cannot talk about the history of a phenomenon without first establishing its nature, varieties, and importance. And for that reason I have saved most of my historical reflections for the last section.

I am indebted to a great number of people for expert advice, for encouragement, for conversation, both relevant and irrelevant. I am most indebted to those who have read portions of the manuscript: Roger B. Wilkenfeld, Milton R. Stern, and Charles McLaughlin at an early stage, Alan Wilde when the manuscript was nearly complete. The penultimate draft was written with the aid of a Summer Research Grant from Temple University. Some of the ideas presented here were first discussed in *Western Humanities Review* and *Journal of General Education*. I am grateful to the editors of those journals for the opportunity to try out my ideas in their pages.

Spring 1970

I
Theory

1
The Argument of the Chapter—
Categorical

"REALLY, universally, relations stop nowhere," wrote Henry James in his Preface to *Roderick Hudson*, "and the exquisite problem of the artist is eternally but to draw, by a geometry of his own, the circle within which they shall happily *appear* to do so. He is in the perpetual predicament that the continuity of things is the whole matter, for him, of comedy and tragedy; that this continuity is never, by the space of an instant or an inch, broken, and that, to do anything at all, he has at once intensely to consult and intensely to ignore it." [1]

It is not only fiction, of course, that must end. All art ends—music with silence, the painting with its frame or its wall, literature of any genre at least with the covers of the book. Just as obviously nearly all art adapts itself to the condition of its having to end. It must *seem* to end, in other words, and though this fundamental necessity is sometimes bypassed and subverted—in deliberately fragmentary poems, for example, and in those mannerist paintings in which an element of the composition actually escapes the frame—the audacity, often the self-consciousness, with which the appearance of ending is avoided simply confirms the strength of the compulsion to end.

Robert M. Adams has argued for the existence and validity

[1] *The Art of the Novel: Critical Prefaces by Henry James* (New York: Scribners, 1934), p. 5.

of what he calls "open form." [2] The tensions of many works
are unresolved, their forms unenclosed, and there is no reason
why they should be otherwise, if the reader grants their implicit purposes. *The Sound and the Fury*, by William Faulkner, is intentionally open, Adams maintained, as indeed is
most modern fiction. Yet to call attention to the possibilities
of formal openness is not to say that such works do not end
or are not made to seem to end. No one is purged at the end
of Ibsen's *Ghosts*, another of Adams' examples, but neither
does anyone remain in his seat waiting for another act. A
formal enclosure, or an unwillingness to enclose, takes place
at many levels, and even though a work may remain open
at a number of levels, still some of the most ingenious exer-
cises of a writer's craft may serve to persuade us that his
work is finished.

It is the special fate of the artist in extended prose, however, that some kind of accommodation must be made between "the continuity of things," as James put it, and the
"geometry" of art, not simply once but many times, since
nearly every narrative work of any length proceeds from beginning to end by the route of its subordinate beginnings and
endings. The novelist's problem is perhaps not different in
kind from that of the dramatist or the writer of extended narrative poetry, but it is different in degree and intensity. For
the central tradition of the novel represents a search for
artistic equivalents of change and continuity, of the amplitude and variety of experience, in a way that narrative poetry
and the drama seldom do.

As the one genre which most consistently displays an
awareness of time in its minutely ordinary passage, it is especially paradoxical that traditionally this very temporal con-

[2] *Strains of Discord: Studies in Literary Openness* (Ithaca, N.Y.:
Cornell University Press, 1958).

tinuity should be so frequently interrupted. Thirty-seven times in *The Wings of the Dove* white space interrupts its richly detailed continuity, in *Vanity Fair* sixty-seven times, and in *Don Quixote* one hundred twenty-six. Although *continuity* must have meant something vastly different to the author of *Lazarillo de Tormes*, to Fielding, to Sterne, to Galsworthy, and to the Joyce of *Finnegans Wake*, yet for each, to make a continuous prose fiction was to make it out of partly discrete, partly enclosed units. Of a principle so nearly universal, so apparently central to the purposes of fiction, it is worth asking why. But properly, an inquiry into the theory of narrative division should begin not with the special demands of the novel but with those general conditions of extended narration in which the novel, for all of its peculiar pressures, is similar to other narrative forms.

One way of beginning to answer the questions implied by the fact of narrative division is by observing the relations between responses to experience and responses to art. Everyone recognizes psychological similarities and differences between the two. Nothing in experience moves an observer in the way that tragedy, symphonic music, or sculpture do. Still, it is no simplification of the complexities of art to find that most of one's responses to art—narrative art in particular—are either identical or analogous to one's responses to experience: affection and antipathy, boredom and interest, pleasure and pain, curiosity and indifference.

Every critical approach to literature, though sometimes in implicit and unacknowledged ways, begins with the prior fact of the mind, accustomed to respond to experience in certain ways, and thus predisposed to respond in certain analogous ways to works of art. Of these analogous responses perhaps none is more important—in experience, in art, and in the relation between the two—than the impulse to shape materials into intelligible and satisfying forms. In both the perception of experience and the response to art, one seeks to enclose, to perform the act which, at its simplest, is that basic gestalt formation by which an observer sees three dots and perceives the possibility that they may become corners of a triangle. An observer of the sky separates figure from ground and perceives that one group of stars resembles a "W" and another group of stars resembles a crab. An observer sees a depression in the earth, contrasts the depression with its surrounding plane, and makes it a gestalt by calling it a "hole." As Wolfgang Köhler points out, built into every language are hundreds of words which refer to this pattern-making faculty: brink, edge, beginning, end, close, piece, part, rest, remainder, proceeding, finishing, continuing, deviating, retarding, and so on.[3]

The particular ways in which pattern formation takes place are determined, of course, by education, by culture, and by individual differences, as is borne out by anthropological reports, for example, on the inability of African natives to "see" motion pictures or the large number of words in Eskimo languages for *snow*. Yet gestalt formation, as a perceptual act, is universal, since all cultures provide evidence of its performance and all languages provide mechanisms for its expression. The impulse to enclose, in short, is a basic property of the mind, inseparable from man's humanness. Consequently, the shaping of narratives into patterns is simply the ineluctable result of the universal human perceptual modes that lie at the basis of that shaping act.

Theories of gestalt perception are a convenient, accessible means for arriving at the same conclusions which can be reached by other routes. Wilhelm Worringer, for example, posits the two poles of abstraction and empathy as the ex-

[3] *Gestalt Psychology* (New York: Liveright, 1947), p. 204.

tremities between which all art lies. "The primal artistic impulse," he says,

has nothing to do with the rendering of nature. It seeks after pure abstraction as the only possibility of repose within the confusion and obscurity of the world-picture, and creates out of itself, with instinctive necessity, geometric abstraction. It is the consummate expression, and the only expression of which man can conceive, of emancipation from all the contingency and temporality of the world-picture.[4]

By wresting the artistic object out of the world at large, Worringer continues, man purifies it and makes it independent of time, of its physical context, and of its observer. To extend Worringer's argument, narrative art in most of its forms tends toward the pole of empathy. We are encouraged to see the artistic work as being, in certain ways, an extension of experience at large, and we are encouraged to enter into the work and respond to it with some degree of personal involvement.

Yet the anxieties and uncertainties of the world view which lie behind the primal impulse to abstraction never entirely disappear from any culture. No art, however empathic its orientation, is without its element of abstraction, since that element of abstraction is capable of lending to art which is not abstract some of the clarity of outline, independence, and intelligibility which pure, geometric abstraction contains.

Since much of narrative art transfers from experience into art complexity of surface, temporal flow, and the confusions of context, it is especially likely that narrative art will seek to shape its uncertainties into units perceivable more or less as abstractions—perceivable, to borrow a metaphor from

[4] *Abstraction and Empathy: A Contribution to the Psychology of Style*, trans. Michael Bullock (New York: International Universities Press, 1953), p. 44.

Worringer's dichotomy, as circles, squares, and triangles. (James writes, of *The Awkward Age*, "Though the relations of a human figure or a social occurrence are what make such objects interesting, they also make them, to the same tune, difficult to isolate, to surround with the sharp black line, to frame in the square, the circle, the charming oval, that helps any arrangement of objects to become a picture." [5]) To say that highly empathic art still retains some of the impulse to shape its materials into clear, independent, abstract forms is only a slightly more devious way of saying that man is that animal which seeks to enclose. Narrative art can hardly escape that human impulse.

It is not similarities between experience and art so much as differences that interest Susanne Langer when she argues that in comparison with the intelligible, organic form in art, "actual experience has no such closed form. It is usually ragged, unaccentuated, so that irritations cut the same figure as sacrifices, amusements rank with high fulfillments, and casual human contacts seem more important than the beings behind them." Such a distinction is useful though perhaps overstated. "Ragged" as experience may be, one still goes through life separating with considerable clarity print from page, speech from silence, garden from yard, a recognizable face from a group photograph, a trip from its preparation and completion, Wednesday from Tuesday and Thursday. Mrs. Langer continues: "But there is a normal and familiar condition which shapes experience into a distinct mode, under which it can be apprehended and valued: that is memory. Past experience, as we remember it, takes on form and character, shows us persons instead of vague presences and their utterances, and modifies our impressions by knowledge of things that came after, things that change one's spontaneous

[5] *The Art of the Novel*, p. 101.

evaluation." [6] It is in this mode of virtual memory, she says, that literature operates. Yet, if pattern formation is more frequently possible and judgments more reliable in memory and the virtual memory of art, these patterns are not essentially different from those that one seeks to make, with somewhat less success, in immediate experience.

The esthetics of Worringer and Mrs. Langer provide different perspectives toward the patterning of fiction from the formulations of gestalt psychology introduced earlier. And the criticism of Frank Kermode provides another such perspective, or perhaps more properly a multitude of such perspectives. For in Kermode's view, the shaping of novels is inseparable from the shaping which we give to our fictions—taking fictions in the widest possible sense—our myths, our philosophies of history, our imagination of crisis, cycle, apocalypse. That Sartre, for example, plays with beginnings and endings in his fiction, leading the reader into false expectations, is a matter of significant philosophical import. The largeness of Kermode's criticism makes it possible for him to relate world view to the making of fiction since they are both, in the long run, part of the same activity. [7] Thus the making of chapters can be placed in a number of philosophical and esthetic contexts. The formulations of gestalt psychology are reconcilable to any of these—not an explanation, but a metaphor, a common denominator.

If the pattern-forming impulse is universal, both in experience and in art, it is not always capable of fulfillment. In the rather thin ground which surrounds Cassiopeia, one can easily separate the constellation. Within the Milky Way, it is all but impossible to discern separate figures. Beyond a certain

[6] *Feeling and Form* (New York: Scribners, 1953), pp. 262–63.
[7] *The Sense of an Ending: Studies in the Theory of Fiction* (New York: Oxford University Press, 1967).

point, if the raw data of experience are numerous enough and indistinguishable enough, the gestalt perception fails. The attraction of a jigsaw puzzle in which all of the pieces are colored red is, of course, just this difficulty, the near impossibility of seeing patterns. To shift from experience to art, an observer, from a single point in space and in a rather short period of time, can respond to most paintings—even one so crowded as, say, a historical panorama by David—as a satisfyingly enclosed gestalt.

In the case of extended narrative, this capacity to respond directly to the formal enclosure of a work is frustrated by those qualities that make it all but impossible to see figures and grounds in the Milky Way. Extended narrative is experienced at length, and thus it far exceeds most paintings, most sculptures, most lyric poems in the sheer bulk of its detail. The classic description of this inability to experience extended narrative directly is in the eloquent first page of Percy Lubbock's book, *The Craft of Fiction*, a passage that shifts the problems of a dense and intractable continuity from the creative process, as James describes it, to the perceptive process of the reader and critic.

To grasp the shadowy and fantasmal form of a book, to hold it fast, to turn it over and survey it at leisure—that is the effort of a critic of books, and it is perpetually defeated. Nothing, no power, will keep a book steady and motionless before us, so that we may have time to examine its shape and design. As quickly as we read, it melts and shifts in the memory; even at the moment when the last page is turned, a great part of the book, its finer detail, is already vague and doubtful. A little later, after a few days or months, how much is really left of it? A cluster of impressions, some clear points emerging from a mist of uncertainty, this is all we can hope to possess, generally speaking, in the name of a book. . . . Nobody would venture to criticize a building, a statue, a picture, with nothing before him but the memory of a single glimpse caught in passing; yet the critic of literature, on the whole, has to found his opinion upon little more.[8]

The short story can be read in a sitting. Both in its classic theory and in its practice, the short story seeks to achieve an economy and unity of form which enable the reader to experience it as, in fact, a gestalt. James was fond of speaking of the short novel as "the shapely nouvelle," suggesting that even at the length of forty or fifty pages, a narrative is capable of being so managed as to enable the reader to respond directly to its form, in its entirety. But narrative of the length of epic, romance, and novel exceeds the limits of the reader's pattern-making faculty. Perhaps the ideal reader of extended narrative is one who reads the work at a single sitting, without diversion and without interruption. But even if this were frequently done, it is not at all likely that the frustrations which Percy Lubbock describes would be prevented.

If art, in general, demands in creator and observer a heightening of the gestalt perception which organizes experience itself, then the writer of extended narrative is obliged to make his work out of subordinate, distinguishable parts, each of which can be seen in its relation to the whole work and each of which can be seen as a form in itself. Thus the writer induces anticipations which can be fulfilled at different levels: days which begin and end, alliances which are made and broken, locations which are visited temporarily, antagonists who are vanquished. Since the bulk of a narrative work exceeds one's capacity to respond directly to its formal enclosure, one sees the pattern of the whole work—the moral education of the hero or the vicissitudes of a love affair—by seeing its subordinate configurations in turn. Or, to put it

[8] *The Craft of Fiction* (London: Jonathan Cape, 1921), pp. 1–2.

another way, one responds to the form of an epic by responding to the successive forms of its books; one responds to the form of a novel by responding to its chapters. Without the possibility of responding to the form of its chapters, as more-or-less discrete units, an understanding of the whole work would be infinitely more difficult than it now is.

Of these subordinate configurations, the writer has several theoretical options open to him. In later chapters we shall see how, in all their complication and amplitude, these theoretical options are realized in fiction. For the moment, such options will be sketched in a bare, paradigmatic form.

First, the writer can present the data of his book, or chapter, or episode, along with their enclosure. In terms of gestalt psychology, the writer here gives us three dots and then proceeds to show us, by drawing a line, how his three dots form a triangle. The simplest narrative form of such an option is the fable, in which the narrative enclosure is reinforced by the addition of the moral. But even in narratives far more complex than the fable, deliberateness of enclosure is by no means rare.

Secondly, the writer can present the materials of an apparent gestalt but enclose these materials in a way different from our expectations. Here the writer gives us three dots, but just as we expect the drawing of a triangle, he surprises us and connects the dots by means of a curve instead. Max Wertheimer has defined critical intelligence as "the process of destroying one gestalt in favor of a better one," [9] a definition capable, certainly, of referring to aspects of the narrative imagination. James Thurber once wrote a series of fables in which this option is exercised in some kind of pure form, the apparent point of each fable being supplanted by another point

[9] Quoted in R. W. Gerard, "The Biological Basis of Imagination," *The Scientific Monthly*, LXII (June, 1946), 483.

—ironic, slightly silly, but not without its own rationale. Wertheimer's definition reminds us that such play with the significance of a narrative unit is a property both of ironic fables and of fiction of the most complex and sophisticated kind.

Third, the writer can provide us with materials suggesting the means for their enclosure yet withholding from us the enclosure itself. Here he gives us three dots and ends his presentation, leaving us with the responsibility for recognizing the possibility of a triangle if we wish. There is rarely very much, for instance, in the individual chapters of Henry James's fiction that tells us with any explicitness what the chapter means at any level of action, of theme, of structure, though there is always material enough so that we can infer such significance if we wish.

Fourth, the writer can present us with materials which suggest an ambiguity of enclosures. Here he gives us an irregular sprinkling of dots. We may experiment, if we wish, with lines and curves and figures, but any enclosure which we make is uncertain, subjective, and arbitrary, like interpretations of Rorschach ink-blots. Such configural suspension is the avowed aim, for example, of Robbe Grillet.

In each of these four situations, an order and a shape is imposed upon events in time; it is this order which is the rationale of the chapter. Even in the fourth case, an ordered succession of bafflements is intelligible in a way that a long and undistinguishable sequence of ambiguity is not. A series of Rorschach ink-blots is intelligible in a way that a long, irregular smear of ink is not, even though the individual ink-blots provide no clues to their proper enclosure.

More than intelligibility, clarity, a heightened sense of meaning, and a satisfaction of the need for order, however, the division of a long narrative provides a purely esthetic pleasure, one of the few comparatively abstract pleasures which an art so little abstract as narrative art can provide. Kenneth Burke writes of the categorical expectations which one brings to art of all kinds. One begins a sonnet expecting that it will contain fourteen lines in one of several metrical arrangements; one begins Pope expecting couplets, end stops, the caesura; one begins an epic expecting an invocation, expanded metaphors, a poetic use of names. Contrary to those expectations which arise during the reading of a work, categorical expectations exist anterior to the reading. As these expectations are fulfilled, they provide what Burke calls the appeal of "conventional form," the appeal "of form *as form.*" Burke cites the example of "the final Beethoven rejoicing of a Beethoven finale." "The audience 'awaits' it," Burke writes, "before the first bar of the music has been played." [10]

At least since Homer, readers of extended narratives have expected categorically that such works will be divided, that they will contain within their beginnings and ends a series of subordinate beginnings and endings. Jane Austen begins a chapter of *Emma* thus: "The hair was curled, and the maid sent away, and Emma sat down to think and be miserable. It was a wretched business, indeed!" [11] If part of the pleasure one finds in those two sentences is in the ironic juxtaposition of the curling of hair and the onset of misery, part of one's pleasure may also derive from the perception that the ancient art of beginning a new episode has been carried off with consummate skill.

Susanne Langer has writen of the impulse—the necessity really—of composing the chapters of experience as an act of understanding. She cites a passage of D. H. Lawrence's *Sons and Lovers* in which Mrs. Morel must compose events be-

[10] *Counterstatement* (Los Altos, Calif.: Hermes, 1953), pp. 126–27.

[11] Ed. R. W. Chapman (Oxford: Clarendon, 1923), p. 134.

fore she can cope with them. "For a while she could not control her consciousness; mechanically she went over the last scene, then over it again, certain phrases, certain moments coming each time like a brand red-hot down on her soul; and each time she enacted again the past hour, each time the brand came down at the same points, till the mark was burnt in, and the pain burnt out, and at last she came to herself." "Life," Mrs. Langer continues "is incoherent unless we give it form. Usually the process of formulating our own situations and our own biography is not as conscious as Mrs. Morel's struggle to conceive the outrage she suffered; but it follows the same pattern—we 'put it into words,' tell it to ourselves, compose it in terms of 'scenes,' so that in our minds we can enact all its important moments." [12]

We have learned how to do this, how to arrange and organize experience so as to cope with it emotionally, from all the literature we have ever read, from nursery tales to the most sophisticated fiction. Conversely, every writer has learned from the process Mrs. Langer describes the value of composing his art into intelligible parts when the dimensions of the whole work exceed certain limits that are indefinable but nonetheless quite real.

[12] *Feeling and Form*, p. 400.

2
The Argument of the Chapter—
Practical

THE GREAT English novelists of the eighteenth century faced
the problem of making chapters in rather different ways, and
thus they provide grounds for extending a theory of chapters
into a remarkably full range of technical options. From the
point of view of Anglo-American fiction, those writers were,
of course, great innovators. J. M. S. Tompkins reminds us of
how experimental they were regarded in their own time by
recording the widely held opinion that the novel, by the last
quarter of the century, was played out, its technical possibilities exhausted.[1] It is for their experimental and paradigmatic
place in English fiction that they become inevitable theoretical exhibits. Yet they are exhibits not only of the early
novel but of the novel as a genre. They synthesized the possibilities of romance, history, epic, the domestic drama, and
the tentative fictions of their predecessors, and they established the basic formal techniques of the genre so thoroughly
that for a hundred and fifty years nearly every narrative
strategy of every English novel was strongly influenced or
anticipated by them.

In *Moll Flanders* Defoe makes no apparent chapters; the
novel is typographically continuous. Nevertheless, it does
contain narrative units. One such unit ends in this way:

[1] *The Popular Novel in England*, 1770–1800 (London: Constable,
1932), pp. 4–5.

But this affair had its end too; for after about a year, I found that he did not come so often as usual, and at last he left it off altogether without any dislike or bidding adieu; and so there was an end of that short scene of life, which added no great store to me, only to make more work for repentance.[2]

Clearly such a passage indicates the end of a chapter without the typography of chapters, a perfectly explicit ending—the explicitness of which, however, is blurred by the decision not to make it look like an ending on the page. What Defoe, or rather Moll, summarizes suggests the rationale for such a technique. Moll's life is neither cumulative nor climactic but serial. Her life is composed not of stages in her education or her moral development or her dramatic complication but of episodes which do not have (or seldom have) any necessary causal relation with what follows. A narrative unit in Defoe lasts as long as Moll's particular dramatic situation lasts; when the episode is finished—an affair, a new career, a journey—the narrative unit is finished and a new one begins.

Defoe's lack of structural subtlety is likely to seem a bit unrewarding to the reader, but the point is that some lives are climactic, some cumulative, and some merely serial, and Moll's happens to be one of the last. She gains little insight as the novel proceeds except for the acquisition of cunning that comes with experience. One may prefer to read novels about people who do come to understand themselves as Moll does not, but great numbers of people outside of novels gain little insight into themselves as they live out their lives, and it would be presumptuous to insist that such a life style cannot be adopted to novelistic purposes. Moll is motivated by no transcendent goal toward which she attempts to move in the novel; but again, such a comparatively pur-

[2] *Works*, ed. G. H. Maynadier (New York: Sully and Kleinteich, 1903), VIII, 64.

poseless life style is common enough in experience at large. There is no reason why a novelist should not organize his art according to that mode of self-consciousness. In other words, an episodic organization is as legitimate as any other because one way of ordering both experience and art is to see them as a succession of episodes. Birth, marriage, death, accusation, exoneration, renunciation—events such as these can be real beginnings and endings.

Thus Defoe's technique, with its absence of physical division and its minimum of progressive movement, with its barely differentiated series of loves and losses, crimes and punishments, is a remarkably persuasive mimetic structure, fashioned as it is because that is the way experience is felt. Told purportedly by the old bawd herself, with a maximum of recall and a minimum of finesse, the narrative materials are deployed as they are because that is the degree of formal sophistication which we are entitled to expect of her.

In Richardson's *Clarissa* the nearly discrete episodes that life may contain not only do not provide the organizing principle, as they do in *Moll Flanders*, but Richardson's multiple narration and amplitude of detail modify these divisions so as to make them seem almost not to exist. That is, if the end of an action is contained within a letter from Clarissa, it will probably recur in a letter from Lovelace, perhaps in another letter from Anna Howe, and perhaps the events will be further reflected upon by Jack Belford.

No event is likely to seem very gratifyingly ended in such circumstances. Fielding, writing of epistolary fiction, said: "I know not of any essential difference between this and any other way of writing novels, save only, that by making use of letters the writer is freed from the regular beginnings and conclusions of stories, with some other formalities, in which the reader of taste finds no less ease and advantage than the author himself." [3] As Fielding thus recognized, the separate books within Richardson's novels are arbitrary divisions in which the formal necessity to finish and enclose does not exist. The individual letter contains within its own stylized rhetoric all the beginnings and endings that an epistolary novel ever needs.

This is not to say, however, that dividing a narrative by means of its letters is only a mechanical result of its epistolary realism, that the division itself has nothing to do with the formal effects of the narrative. Midway through a letter to her mother, Clarissa writes:

If I do *not* answer him, he will be made desperate, and think himself justified (tho' I shall not think him so) in resenting the treatment he complains of. If I *do*, and if, in compliment to me, he forbears to resent what he thinks himself intitled to resent, be pleased, Madam, to consider the obligation he will suppose he lays me under.

The same letter ends thus:

And so leaving the whole to your own wisdom, and whether you chuse to consult my Papa and Uncles upon this humble application, or not; or whether I shall be allowed to write an answer to Mr. Lovelace, or not (And if allowed so to do, I beg your direction, by whom to send it); I remain, *Honoured Madam*,
Your unhappy, but ever-dutiful Daughter,
CL. HARLOWE [4]

The stylized rhetoric of eighteenth-century correspondence provides the letter with its own resolution. Indeed, probably no other unit of prose ends so conclusively and satisfyingly as the archaic epistolary form, with its syntactic continuity

---

[3] "Preface to *The Familiar Letters*," *Works*, Henley edition (New York: Crosscup & Sterling, 1903), XVI, 20.
[4] *Clarissa*, Shakespeare Head Edition (Oxford: Blackwell, 1930), I, 171, 172.

with the signature. Yet the letter itself could not have been more inconclusive. With its qualifications and parentheses, its piled-up conditional clauses, the letter is a masterful representation of uncertainty. Thus, in the tension between formal units which begin and end hundreds of times and a psychological content which never ends, Richardson builds a formal structure of great power. Formally, *Clarissa* expresses the agonies of stopping and starting, of waiting until tomorrow, of waiting for replies, of asking deliverance, and expressing resignation. In short, it is in part because the individual letters of *Clarissa* each must end, and because they do so with such power, that the novel achieves a sustained and continuously tragic suspense.

Fielding is the first and one of the very few English novelists to theorize about chapter division, but his theory comes in a chapter of *Joseph Andrews* which is so arch, so puzzlingly ironic, that it leaves quite unclear what Fielding meant to assert. The common reader, he begins, may imagine that the division of a narrative is intended only "to swell our Works to a much larger Bulk than they would otherwise be extended to." On the contrary, divisions are for the convenience of the reader, not the author. A space between chapters may be regarded as "an Inn or Resting-Place," and thus may give occasion for a retrospective reflection on the preceding chapter. A work without such occasions for rest and reflection "resembles the Opening of Wilds or Seas, which tires the Eye and fatigues the Spirit when entered upon."

Secondly, chapter division gives the author an opportunity for inscribing at the beginning of a chapter what is to come. Chapter divisions, moreover, prevent the dog-earing of a book. And besides, they have the sanction of antiquity, since Homer and Virgil divided their epics into books. Fielding's chapter on chapters ends with this metaphor: "it becomes an Author generally to divide a Book, as it does a butcher to joint his Meat, for such Assistance is of great Help to both the Reader and the Carver." [5]

Certainly Fielding's final metaphor is ironic, as is his image of Homer bringing out the *Odyssey* book by book, hawking each one separately. Yet it is difficult to assume that the entire chapter is flippant. Fielding's initial point—that chapter division permits rest and reflection while the absence of division results in a kind of spiritual fatigue—makes perfect sense when esthetic principles are reasoned by psychological values. The idea is not unlike the principle discussed in the preceding chapter, the need for limiting the size of the fictional unit to the capacity of the reader's pattern-making faculty. (Fielding's idea, incidentally, is also rather like Poe's animadversions on the long poem in "The Poetic Principle.")

Evidence of Fielding's seriousness, however, lies finally in his practice, for he does seem often to divide his narrative according to the duration of attention which he can legitimately ask of his readers. His chapters are often rather arbitrarily ended units which are over when it is time for narrator and reader (and perhaps the characters themselves) to reflect on what has just happened. A chapter from *Tom Jones*, for example, involves the identity of Mrs. Waters, reflection on the Man of the Hill, Partridge's rustic wit, the belligerence of a sergeant, the effects of a considerable quantity of alehouse liquor, the appearance of Sophia, and so on. It is the kind of chapter which could go on for many times its length. But it ends after just about as many pages as any chapter in Fielding's writings, with these reflections.

[5] *Joseph Andrews*, Wesleyan Edition, ed. Martin Battestin (Middletown, Conn.: Wesleyan University Press, 1967), pp. 89–92.

The beauty of Jones highly charmed her [Mrs. Waters'] eye; but, as she could not see his heart, she gave herself no concern about it. She could feast heartily at the table of love, without reflecting that some other already had been, or hereafter might be, feasted with the same repast. A sentiment which, if it deals but little in refinement, deals however much in substance; and is less capricious, and perhaps less ill-natured and selfish than the desires of those females who can be contented enough to abstain from the possession of their lovers, provided they are sufficiently satisfied that no one else possesses them.[6]

After all the mock sententiousness and misapplied learning, the misunderstood intentions and the language gone wrong, the passionate earnestness and the calculated insincerity of the chapter, it is time to get back to Jones, to his temptations, his love, and to the nature of woman. It is not that the chapter is an episode in any conventional sense of the word, with its own beginning, middle, and its own inevitable end; it is not that it ends out of any internal necessity. It has simply gone on long enough, and before the reader has a chance to become fatigued it is time to induce him to reflect and permit him to rest. Such a chapter makes only the most fragile of gestalts, but there is still a certain configural validity in the kind of chapter which might be entitled "Many Things Happened Which Are Here Related."

The foregoing is not to say that Fielding's chapter divisions are all so arbitrary as the one here described or that chapters exist only for the accommodation of the reader's interest. In fact, Fielding's technique is so various that it provides a broad range of justifications for the chapter. Certainly it is possible to change a scene more conveniently between chapters, as Fielding usually does, than within them. And it is possible to omit irrelevant periods of time between chapters

[6] *Tom Jones* (Baltimore: Penguin, 1966), p. 461.

more easily than to offer a perfunctory summary at mid-chapter, again as Fielding usually does.

It is possible for Fielding to use a chapter break for an adjustment of his tone, and thus the modulations from the narrator's discussions of his art in Fielding's prolegomenous chapters to his narrative proper, from the broad irony of a chapter on Partridge to the narrative intensity of a chapter on Sophia in distress—these adjustments and modulations are made considerably easier by the presence of chapters. *Tom Jones*, too, as many critics have said and as Fielding himself remarked (p. 201), is a structure of contrasts. The chapter title "in which Master Blifil and Jones appear in different lights" is a characteristic one. We are expected, as we read Fielding's fiction, to see people and events "in different lights," to see what was in contrast with what is, to see reality in contrast with its guises. Such a structure of contrasts is more easily built with the flexibility of frequent chapter divisions.

Finally, as Andrew Wright has remarked,[7] Fielding often presents the reader with a "tableau," a comparatively static, almost "posed" picture, in the manner of Hogarth—Joseph naked before the occupants of the stage coach, Tom discovered in the grove with Molly, Booth in prison. It is a narrative technique which can be imagined as existing, perhaps, in a completely continuous narration. But it is difficult to imagine it as being so successful as it is when the tableau is roughly coexistent with the limits of the chapter in which it appears.

So far we have seen that novelists, at least eighteenth-century novelists, may write in chapters because experience itself can be viewed as if it consisted of chapters, because the

[7] *Henry Fielding: Mask and Feast* (Berkeley: University of California Press, 1965), pp. 122–25.

alternating frustrations and fulfillments of life can be given a powerfully dramatic form simply by the act of segmenting the narrative, because the attention and the imagination of the reader are adaptable to small narrative units rather than to long, unbroken ones, and because the technical demands of writing a novel, with its scenic shifts and its omissions are more easily met when the narrative is divided. None of these reasons apply to Sterne. Life, in *Tristram Shandy*, is not lived in episodes.

My mother, you must know—but I have fifty things more necessary to let you know first—I have a hundred difficulties which I have promised to clear up, and a thousand distresses and domestic misadventures crouding in upon me thick and three-fold, one upon the neck of another—a cow broke in (to-morrow morning) to my uncle *Toby*'s fortifications, and eat up two ratios and a half of dried grass, tearing up the sods with it, which faced his horn-work and covered way. *Trim* insists upon being tried by a court-martial—the cow to be shot—*Slop* to be *crucifix'd*—myself to be *tristram'd*, and at my very baptism made a martyr of—poor unhappy devils that we all are! [8]

By his chapter divisions, Sterne achieves a large range of comic effects; but his comic effects are made at the deliberate expense of the conventional advantages of narrative division. Rather than intensifying the dramatic progression of his novel by dividing it, Sterne dissipates its drama. Chapters in *Tristram Shandy* are a few lines long, others nearly interminable, all with little of the apparent regard which Fielding expresses for the reader's interest. While the technical demands Sterne makes for himself are considerable, they are so unconventional as to constitute a parody of conventional technique. One chapter ends, "Imagine to yourself—but this had better

[8] *Tristram Shandy*, ed. James A. Work (New York: Odyssey, 1940), p. 235.

begin a new chapter." And the next chapter begins: "CHAP. IX. Imagine to yourself a little, squat, uncourtly figure of a Doctor *Slop* . . . (p. 104).

At the end of *Middlemarch*, George Eliot suggests that every end is at the same time a beginning. Sterne does her one better. What his manipulation of the chapter suggests is a use of chapters to indicate a distrust of chapters, more than a recognition of beginnings in ends, a denial of the reality of the narrative unit. Time after time, what looks like an episode is no episode, what looks like a digression is no digression. What such an internal, associationist, apparently capricious organization effects is precisely that radical reorientation of the configural mechanism which is possible in fiction, in this case by playing the mind of Tristram against the conventions of fiction.

Without its chapters, no doubt, *Tristram Shandy* would be less funny and quite likely unreadable. And without its chapters, the appearance, which Sterne carefully induces, of an anxious Tristram wrestling with his intractable material would be lost. But finally, Sterne can write chapters of such comic exuberance precisely because his use of a convention in which he does *not* believe indicates with full ironic amplitude the view of the mind, anti-conventional, anti-traditional, and eminently un-chaptered, in which he *does* believe.

The eighteenth-century novelists represent the technique of the chapter come full circle, from an apparent unawareness of its usefulness to a full exploitation of its power and its variety to a parody of it. In one sense there is nothing more to be said about the chapter as an aspect of fictional technique. The beginnings and endings, the technical shifts, the relations between chapters in Jane Austen's novels alone are so subtle and various as to justify a book in themselves. But her chapters do rather little which was not latent in the technical virtuosity of the eighteenth century. In another sense, however, the novelists of the nineteenth century used the chapter in a way which was beyond the concerns, in fact beyond the imagination, of the eighteenth-century novelists.

Wilhelm Dilthey writes of four stages of historical under-standing: first, the addition of explanation to simple narra-tion; second, "the *methodical application of the systematic* human studies to the *explanation* of the historical context"; third, a stage of historiographic method new in the eighteenth century, a tendency to divide the stream of history "*into individual* contexts like those of law, religion, poetry, em-braced by the unity of an age." Dilthey's fourth stage is beyond the historical imagination of the eigtheenth century, and in a roughly analogous way, it is beyond its fictional imagination as well. Dilthey describes the principle of devel-opment in historiography in this way: "A new fundamental characteristic is contained in a historical course of interac-tions, namely that, according to its inner nature, it traverses a series of changes each of which is only possible on the basis of the previous one." [9] Like the historians, novelists in the eighteenth century learned how to make their characters grow and change; they learned, in James's word, to make them "emerge"; they learned how to reveal the pressure of environment. Those new causal and developmental concerns are intimately related to the way in which novels are divided.

In *Middlemarch*, for example, the chapters concerned with Dorothea perform the function of drops in the Chinese water torture. They gradually alter the personality of Dorothea, providing the mechanism by which she grows from adoles-cence to maturity and changes from ingenuousness to despair. We see her maturing, perhaps without being quite sure how

[9] *Pattern and Meaning in History: Thoughts on History and Society,* ed. H. P. Rickman (New York: Harper, 1962), pp. 142–44.

the illusion of growth is being maintained, yet aware, all the same, that the appearance of change is the result of stages, interior crises, and small progressions, the kind of rhythm for which chapter division is indispensible. It is difficult to imagine how the stages and degrees of Dorothea's change could have been crystalized and presented convincingly without the adaptation of the old typographical conventions of the chapter to George Eliot's new developmental purposes.

The early chapters of *The Way of All Flesh*, by Samuel Butler, build up, layer by layer, the genetic and environmental enclosure from which Ernest cannot escape. Again, it is difficult to imagine how that sense of heavy impenetrability could have been evoked by the author without the structural possibilities of chaptered narration.

In *The Aspern Papers*, by Henry James, one has the sense of growing familiarity with the nameless narrator who reveals himself, by stages, as he becomes more involved in his personal intrigue, more deeply and opportunistically committed to his quest for the papers; at the same time, the reader follows those small events that mark the breakdown of reserve in Miss Tita, the narrator's intermediary, as well as those other small events that mark the growth of understanding in Miss Bordereau, the possessor of the papers and the dead poet's aged lover. It is not that chapter division interrupts the tale; it makes the narration possible.

In a famous passage on the responsibilities of the novelist, Virginia Woolf wrote:

Examine for a moment an ordinary mind on an ordinary day. The mind receives a myriad impressions—trivial, fantastic, evanescent, or engraved with the sharpness of steel. From all sides they come, an incessant shower of innumerable atoms; and as they fall, as they shape themselves into the life of Monday or Tuesday, the accent falls differently from of old; the moment of importance came not here but there; so that, if a writer were a free man and not a slave, if he could write what he chose, not what he must, if he could base his work upon his own feelings and not upon convention, there would be no plot, no comedy, no tragedy, no love interest or catastrophe in the accepted style, and perhaps not a single button sewn on as the Bond Street tailors would have it. Life is not a series of gig-lamps symmetrically arranged; life is a luminous halo, a semi-transparent envelope surrounding us from the beginning of consciousness to the end. Is it not the task of the novelist to convey this varying, this unknown and uncircumscribed spirit, whatever aberration or complexity it may display, with as little mixture of the alien and external as possible? We are not pleading merely for courage and sincerity; we are suggesting that the proper stuff of fiction is a little other than custom would have us believe it.[10]

It is a noble passage though not without a certain pathos, for surely one of the operative phrases is "if he would write what he chose, not what he must." Although the emphasis of the passage is on the relation of life to fiction, implicit in it is a reminder of the relation of fiction to reader with its corollary of the responsibilities of the novelist to make his own adjustment to certain broadly esthetic and specifically narrative conventions. Of these, the convention of the chapter, limiting though it may seem to be when seen through a particular view of experience, has arisen and continued through so many kinds of prose fiction because it serves rather than hinders the purpose which Virginia Woolf proposed for fiction. More than a way of making the narrative intelligible, the chapter is a device which enables the narrative to convey the novelist's unique vision.

[10] "Modern Fiction," *Collected Essays* (London: Hogarth, 1966), II, 106.

II
Conventions

3
Cadence

THE HISTORY of prose fiction is full of examples of atypical books. English fiction within a hundred years shows *Tristram Shandy* and *The Monk, Castle Rackrent* and *Nightmare Abbey, Wuthering Heights* and *Pickwick Papers*—each of these, and many more one could name, not altogether independent of tradition but still quite unlike anything that had come before. Prose fiction since the seventeenth century, in fact, is so dominated by the atypical that the genre resists the application of concepts of typicality. In a genre in which the tensions between tradition and individual talent are so frequently resolved rather heavily in favor of individual talent, it is natural that criticism of that genre should so often direct itself toward the vision of the individual writer, in all of its uniqueness, at the significance of his myths and the shape of his imagined world.

But this least conventional of the arts has its conventions all the same. We saw in the preceding section that the very fact of the chapter is a convention of pervasive importance to the art of fiction, and we shall see in later chapters how the division of any given fiction is inevitably connected with its unique artistic power. But there are certain subordinate conventions implied in the fact of the chapter, among these the means, some of them ancient and traditional, by which a chapter is made to seem to end.

One of the chapters of *Vanity Fair* ends thus:

The sun was just rising as the march began—it was a gallant sight—the band led the column, playing the regimental march—then came the Major in command, riding upon Pyramus, his stout charger—then marched the grenadiers, their Captain at their head; in the centre were the colours borne by the senior and junior Ensigns—then George came marching at the head of his company. He looked up, and smiled at Amelia, and passed on; and even the sound of the music died away.[1]

Thackeray's last paragraph is appropriate to the subject matter and tone of his chapter, a pleasantly ironic treatment, among other things, of military duty and honor. Yet Thackeray's paragraph does more than simply finish the chapter in a way that is consistent with its substance. The paragraph contains within itself its own movement, its own beginning, middle, and end. And thus, whatever the degree of resolution which the sense of the last paragraph provides for the larger patterns of the chapter, Thackeray's last paragraph, with its own skilfully decisive rhetoric, provides its own interior sense of ending.

First there is the image of the passing parade with its passing reinforced by the fading sound of the band. The paragraph, secondly, includes a long and complex series, ending with the magnificently anticlimactic appearance of George. The imagery of the parade, moreover, has a peculiarly staged effect, a theatrical quality suggested by the phrase "gallant sight" and by its insistent dashes. But this quality

[1] The passage occurs at the end of Chapter XXX. Beginning in this chapter, extensive quotations will be made either from the ends of chapters or from the beginnings. Since none of the excerpts poses any real problem in location, full documentation will be omitted; only the chapter and novel are indicated, except in those few cases in which there are no chapter numbers or in which a translation is relevant to the identification of a passage.

of rhetorical excess which makes Thackeray's last paragraph
almost a parody of all last paragraphs is balanced not only by
the author's ironies (Pyramus as the name of the Major's
horse) but by the inversion of what must have been, even
in mid-nineteenth century, one of the staler clichés of the
fictional ending—the sunset. Here the parade, the music, the
exchange of parting glances fade not into the setting sun but
into the sunrise.

The passage of the parade is further reinforced by the
coordinate syntax of the last sentence. Three *ands* in succession make a kind of syntactic *tour de force*. It is rarely a
construction which a skilful writer would permit himself in
mid-paragraph or even in mid-chapter. And it is a difficult
construction to follow, suggesting as it does a cumulative
series of coordinate elements. In other words, one might say,
in mid-sentence, "the red, white, and blue"; but one had
better not say "the red, and the white, and the blue" unless
the sentence, or probably the paragraph, is finished. Any
given instance of the construction sounds, by its measured
rhythm and by analogy with other instances of the construction in the same position, like an ending. Finally, the word
even, in the last clause, suggests one last reinforcement of
finality. Thus Thackeray's chapter ends by means of a series
of details placed in such a way and stated in such a manner
as to imply unmistakably that the chapter is over, however
unresolved the chapter as a whole may be.

What happens in Thackeray's last paragraph is that certain
tensions within the whole chapter are resolved, but, more
than this, the formal expectation of an ending is fulfilled as
well. Kenneth Burke's concept of "conventional form" ap-
plies here—the idea that the reader carries to a work certain
formal anticipations before he has even begun to experience

the work. The reader expects that the individual chapters in novels will be so managed that they will seem to offer minor, secondary conclusions.

Such is the norm in fiction. The writer of fiction may choose to end his chapters abruptly, and many writers from Sterne to the present have chosen to do so. But a writer must surely do so in pursuit of a special effect, so widespread is the convention by which a chapter is made to seem to end. Although the simple resolution of certain patterns within a chapter may be enough to give a chapter a satisfyingly conclusive ending, most chapters reinforce this sense of conclusion, as does Thackeray in the example above, by various stylistic and substantive devices which, in certain positions, enable the chapter to seem to end and which can be called, by analogy with music, cadence.

The first chapter of the Book of Job—and it is unmistakably a chapter even though the chapter typography has been supplied by editors—ends first with Job's response to his misfortunes. "Then Job arose, and rent his mantle, and shaved his head, and fell down upon the ground, and worshipped." To delay the spiritual response for which the chapter exists until the external details of Job's grief are named is a masterful touch, whether by the author or the King James translators, thus making Job's piety, when it is described, all the more conclusive. At this point, the chapter is, from the viewpoint of its essential action, ended. But Job comments: "Naked I came out of my mother's womb, and naked shall I return thither: The Lord gave, and the Lord hath taken away." His comments generalize upon his immediate situation; they are balanced, aphoristic, epigrammatic, self-contained, needing no further elaboration. Thus, besides confirming the fact that Job's worship is not shallow or ill-considered, they supply Job's summary of his situation. "Blessed be the name of the Lord," he says. And the narrator adds his assurance to the truth of Job's professions: "In all this Job sinned not, nor charged God foolishly." However resolved or unresolved Job's initial testing in the first chapter may be, the chapter achieves a powerful sense of finality by means of the substance and the syntax of its cadence.

James Joyce, of all novelists, has the least obligation to tailor his narrative to the expectations of his readers or to segment it in traditional ways. Yet for all his indifference to the conventional anticipations of the readers of conventional novels, for all of his transcendence of conventional time and space, *Finnegans Wake* participates in the tradition of cadence—a tradition, as indicated, as old as the Book of Job. What is more, *Finnegans Wake* contains some of the most powerful cadences in all of prose fiction. "The silent cock shall crow at last. The west shall shake the east awake. Walk while ye have the night for morn, lightbreakfastbringer, morroweth whereon every past shall full fost sleep. Amain" (Viking Edition, p. 473).

Here, as elsewhere, Joyce's technique permits a fusion of the realistic and the incantatory, the immediate and the remote, so that his cadences end with a range of levels impossible in more conventional fiction. What is probably the best-known passage in the entire work is the cadence which ends the Anna Livia Plurabelle section.

Can't hear with the waters of. The chittering waters of. Flittering bats, fieldmice bawk talk. Ho! Are you not gone ahome? What Thom Malone? Can't hear with bawk of bats, all thim liffeying waters of. Ho, talk save us! My foos won't moos. I feel as old as yonder elm. A tale told of Shaun or Shem? All Livia's daughtersons. Dark hawks hear us. Night! Night! My ho head halls. I feel as heavy as yonder stone. Tell me of John or Shaun? Who were Shem and Shaun the living sons or daughters of?

Night now! Tell me, tell me, tell me elm! Night night! Telmetale
of stem or stone. Beside the rivering waters of, hitherandthithering
waters of. Night! (pp. 215–16)

If inducing a sense of finality at the end of a narrative unit
is as universal a technique as suggested here—so universal as
to appear in Thackeray, the Book of Job, and Joyce, as well,
presumably to enclose chapters and reinforce their finality—
then it is worth asking how it is that cadences are made.

To begin with the most obvious, a chapter is ordinarily
followed by white space. Even in Virginia Woolf's *Mrs.
Dalloway*, which dispenses with chapters for the sake, perhaps, of presenting an image of intense psychological continuity, a sense of endings and beginnings is still achieved by
skipping an extra line. It is one of the few typographcial
devices which the writer of prose fiction has at his disposal,
and the device always works to the advantage of the writer.
For even if the writer manages the form of his cadence in-
eptly, he achieves a certain sense of conclusion by stopping,
permitting some white space, and beginning a new chapter.
It is difficult for the reader to decide how much of the sense
of conclusion found in an ending is a response to formal
gratification and how much of the sense of conclusion is a
judgment after the fact—the feeling that an episode has
ended because one can *see* that it has ended. The use of white
space, however, is not a cadence, not a device which is a part
of the style and substance of a work, only a physical possibility
of typesetting put in service of the novelist's art.

Of cadences proper, one may begin with the declarative
cadence, in which the narrator simply tells us that the
chapter is over. "Here the Graces think proper to end their
description," wrote Fielding, "and here we think proper to
end the chapter" (*Tom Jones*, IX, v). Hasek ended an episode of *The Good Soldier Schweik*: "And so ended the

administration of extreme unction which didn't come off" (Penguin Edition, I, 13). And Samuel Beckett ended Chapter 6 of *Murphy*, a chapter devoted to Murphy's mind, this way: "This painful duty having now been discharged, no further bulletins will be issued." Declarative cadence, the ending as ending, is generally adaptable to a narrative technique in which an extroverted narrator speaks familiarly to his implied audience with an attitude of mutual trust, as in the case of Fielding and Hasek and to some extent even with Beckett.

To shift perspective somewhat, the finality of a cadence may reside not in the express intention of the narrator but in an event which is finished as the chapter ends.

Henchard's face had become still more stern at these interruptions, and he drank from his tumbler of water as if to calm himself or gain time. Instead of vouchsafing a direct reply, he stiffly observed—

"If anybody will tell me how to turn grown wheat into wholesome wheat I'll take it back with pleasure. But it can't be done."

Henchard was not to be drawn again. Having said this, he sat down.

So ends Chapter 5 of Hardy's *Mayor of Casterbridge*, a chapter which is unmistakably over because its ending contains within it a remarkably final act. Chapters often contain within them speeches, arranged so that the end of the speech coincides with the end of the chapter. Hardy arranged Henchard's speech so as to cancel any expectation of a reply —and reinforced the finality of his speech by describing Henchard's I'll-not-hear-another-word stance.

The parade in the paragraph from Thackeray quoted earlier is such an interior conclusion. As Thackeray's parade passes, fades, ends, the chapter ends, though Thackeray's chapter is ended by the simultaneous operation of several other rhetorical forces. The possibilities for such cadences are unlimited. The painting is finished, the door is locked, the shades are drawn, the performance is over, the sun sets, and the chapter ends. Most frequently the subordinate completion is a small action which is not a necessary resolution of a large pattern but a specific device of the cadence itself.

It is sometimes possible to achieve a sense of finality not by reference to what is ending but by reference to what is to come, an anticipatory cadence. Fielding, again, used such a cadence frequently. "Abigail now made haste to finish the remainder of her meal, and then repaired back to her mistress, when the conversation passed which may be read in the next chapter" (*Tom Jones*, X, iv). A chapter of Butler's *Way of All Flesh* ends: "And now I will continue my story" (Chapter 19). Such a cadence, in the very act of encouraging the reader to look ahead, encourages him as well to see the present chapter as being, at least in part, a completed unit. A masterpiece of this double vision, backwards and forwards, occurs in James's *Aspern Papers*, the end of Chapter I:

"Well, you're a precious pair! Doesn't it occur to you that even if you are able to say you are not Mr. Cumnor in person they may still suspect you of being his emissary?"

"Certainly, and I see only one way to parry that."

"And what may that be?"

I hesitated a moment. "To make love to the niece."

"Ah," cried Mrs. Prest, "wait till you see her!"

The anticipatory cadence flourished most extensively in serialized novels of the nineteenth century, where the success of the novelist often hung not on the success of his whole work so much as the success of his individual chapters in, at best, engaging the reader's continuing imagination or, at worst, titillating him. But in an example such as that from James, the artistic finesse, the irony, and the psychological penetration suggest some of the possibilities latent in that ancient device of inviting the reader to wonder what is going to happen next.

Most travel is a transition from chapter to chapter, uninteresting in itself, and hence the beginning of a journey can become an ending, a scenic cadence. "Pickle commended his resolution, though in his heart, he blessed himself from such a barbarous Goth; and, after they had despatched two or three bottles of his beer, they proceeded on their journey, and arrived in town about eleven at night" (Smollett, *Peregrine Pickle*, Chapter CV). "With this they descended out of the fair, and went onward to the village, where they obtained a night's lodging" (*The Mayor of Casterbridge*, Chapter 3). In *Lazarillo de Tormes* there is scarcely any other kind of cadence; nearly every chapter ends with Lazarillo traveling. Scenic cadence is so classic a device both of conclusion and selection, it is so useful for omitting time and space without seeming to violate continuity, that it appears in fiction of all kinds, though of course it is more predominant in fiction of a broad, inclusive, episodic technique.

A sense of formal completion results from a progression of events leading to a further event or a passage of time which convention has led the reader to expect will not be rendered fictionally. Perhaps the most obvious and conclusive of such progressions is the preparation for sleep. Pepys' "And so to bed," though nonfictional, is a kind of irreducible archetype of the form. Such cadences are often indirect and casual: " 'Of course she'll stop,' said Mrs. Saunders. 'And now, Esther, come along and help me to make you up a bed in the parlour' " (Moore, *Esther Waters*, Chapter XIII). But sleep is not always casually begun, and thus a cadence which ends an episode may on occasion bear a heavy emotional weight, even to the point of melodrama, as seen in Chapter XIII of *David Copperfield*:

I remember how the solemn feeling with which at length I turned my eyes away, yielded to the sensation of gratitude and rest which the sight of the white-curtained bed—and how much more the lying softly down upon it, nestling in the snow-white sheets!—inspired. I remember how I thought of all the solitary places under the night sky where I had slept, and how I prayed that I never might be houseless any more, and never might forget the houseless. I remember how I seemed to float, then, down the melancholy glory of that track upon the sea, away into the world of dreams.

It is, of course, unnecessary that any character in any novel ever go to sleep, and characters in hundreds of novels never do. But as an artifice for rendering the tranquility and the dramatic lapse that chapter division demands and as a device for focusing the fiction, after a passage of complex relationships, upon an individual consciousness, the fictional sleep is infinitely varied, capable of carrying a symbolic weight that stands, somehow, for the substance of the entire chapter. "He stared at the red, shivering reflection of a fire on the white wall of his tent until, exhausted and ill from the monotony of his suffering, he fell asleep" (Crane, *The Red Badge of Courage*, Chapter 2).

"After luncheon they improvised a shelter in order to repose awhile. It was the right thing to do on Nepenthe at that hour of the day, and Mr. Keith tried to conform to custom even under unusual circumstances such as these. Protected by the boat's scarlet awning from the rays of the sun, they slumbered through the flaming hours" (Douglas, *South Wind*, Chapter XXII).

There are a hundred things that human beings do every

day that are rarely shown in novels. Working-class characters in Dickens' fiction, for example, tend to be defined by their occupations, but we rarely see them actually working. Each one of these conventional omissions—eating, working, dressing, reading the newspaper—can be omitted from any novel altogether. But each one of them can also, as in the case of sleep, serve the double function of making the chapter break seem esthetically plausible by leading up to an event which there is every reason to omit and providing the author with an occasion for a summary gesture, often full of symbolic import. For many years sexual activity was seldom rendered fictionally, and even in the early work of D. H. Lawrence, the beginning of intimate sex becomes the ending of a chapter. Yet that ending is a symbolic summary of the significance of the omitted events. "And they crept closer, closer together, hearts beating to one another. And even as the hymn rolled on, they ceased to hear it" (*The Rainbow*, Chapter V).

Less explicit than the preceding cadences but no less sure as an ending is the technique of broadening the scope of the narrative, momentarily expanding its dimensions temporally or philosophically. If the main technique of a chapter, for example, is scenic, the temporal scale within the chapter will be fairly limited. The events of the scene must proceed deliberately, with reference to their immediate complexities and their immediate antecedents. To relate the events of the scene to their remote causes or to speculate on their remote consequences is to break the spell of the scene. Thus only at the end of the scene can the technical and esthetic premises of the scene be transcended successfully. Broadening the time scheme, besides suggesting that the scene is finished, reinforces the mood of retrospective and anticipatory reflection which most novelists almost certainly wish to induce in their readers at the chapter's end. "So they separated softly enough.

She was to be let off hearing about Lord Mark so long as she made it good that she wasn't underhand about any one else. She had denied everything and everyone, she reflected as she went away—and that was a relief; but it also made rather a clean sweep of the future. The prospect put on a bareness that already gave her something in common with the Miss Condrips" (James, *The Wings of the Dove*, Book I, Chapter II). "And the fruition of the whole scheme was such dust and ashes as this" (*The Mayor of Casterbridge*, Chapter XIX).

The scope of a chapter can also be extended at its end by a summary which is not so much temporal in its breadth as philosophical, where the summary induces the reader to reflect not on past and future but on the actors and events of the chapter insofar as they are representative of human beings at large. "Alethea laid herself out to please, as indeed she did wherever she went, and if any woman lays herself out to do this, she generally succeeds" (*The Way of All Flesh*, Chapter XXXIII).

Such extensions of scope as these are quite explicit. At a much more implicit and unobtrusive level, the same summarizing breadth can sometimes be suggested by the use of adverbs and adverbial phrases which intimate a temporal or philosophical breadth. In Jane Austen's *Emma*, for example, these phrases are ordinary enough so that they might well occur any number of times in the novel: "in time," "would be doing nothing," "always," "would be forgotten," "supplanted," "expected," "very early," "never," "now," "too much to hope," "in one year." Yet all of these phrases have a temporal dimension, and when they occur at the end of a chapter, even when the passage that ends the chapter is not, in any ordinary sense, a summary, these words give the effect of assessment to the cadence and hence a subtle feeling of finality. Here is the passage from Chapter III of *Emma*:

In time, of course, Mr. Knightley would be forgotten, that is, supplanted; but this could not be expected to happen very early. Mr. Knightley himself would be doing nothing to assist the cure —not like Mr. Elton. Mr. Knightley, always so kind, so feeling, so truly considerate for every body, would never deserve to be less worshipped than now; and it really was too much to hope even of Harriet, that she could be in love with more than *three* men in one year.

Again and again phrases like these occur in Jane Austen's work, phrases such as "at any time" or "at last," which might well seem extravagant or uncharacteristically hyperbolic in the middle of the chapter but at its end suggest, with the subtlest of rhetorical pressures, that the chapter is over.

If a sense of conclusion can be induced by broadening the scope of the chapter at its end, it can also be induced by narrowing it. The preparation for sleep is such a narrowing of focus. An effect comparable to the reduction of the complexities of a chapter to a single reflective mind is the reduction to a single sensory perception. One of Cora's reflections, in Faulkner's *As I Lay Dying*, ends: "Her hand rises and touches her beads lightly, and then her hair. When she finds me watching her, her eyes go blank" (Modern Library edition, p. 343). One of the passages given to Darl ends: "The wagon moves; the mules' ears begin to bob. Behind us, above the house, motionless in tall and soaring circles, they diminish and disappear" (p. 411). Quite often sections of Faulkner's novel end with smelling, tasting, hearing, and especially seeing, in all of its forms—quite often, and significantly so, a kind of inarticulate stare, a wordless gawk beyond which the chapter cannot go.

Such a narrowing of focus upon a sensory experience is a frequent device in fiction which is subjective and interior. There is not much in common, for example, between *As I Lay Dying* and *The Horse's Mouth*, by Joyce Cary, except for the tendency of each to anchor themes and values to individual perceiving minds. Yet the intensely subjective quality of the fiction of both Faulkner and Cary is enough to insure that their chapters will often end in similar ways. "More in sadness than in anger," reflects Gulley Jimson, Joyce Cary's artist hero. "Because of the bell ringing in my head" (Chapter 11). It is an ambiguous last sentence, suggesting at once Jimson's blood pressure and his clarity of moral vision. Structurally, the last sentence is not ambiguous at all. It brings the chapter to rest at the point which marks the source of the novel's vitality and the center of its values, the inner eye of Jimson.

At an indefinable point, the narrow, intense sensory impressions of a character at the end of a chapter become more than a device for inducing a sense of tranquility and a sense of fundamental, irreducible experience. They become a metaphor for the relation between man and world, a cosmic cadence. In such a case the narrator of the novel generally supplies the sensory impressions which a main character is presumably experiencing, stating them in his, the narrator's, own person. Almost invariably, the form that such cadence takes, in thousands of chapters, is a description, by the narrator, of some aspect of physical nature, in its tranquility and permanence, by way of contrast with the turbulence and impermanence of the rest of the chapter. "Ronny's steps had died away, and there was a moment of absolute silence. No ripple disturbed the water, no leaf stirred" (Forster, *Passage to India*, Chapter 7). "A cloud of dark smoke, as from smoldering ruins, went up toward the sun now bright and gay in the blue, enameled sky" (*The Red Badge of Courage*, Chapter 17). An interesting variation sets the individual against large forces exterior to himself while showing that the character is unaware of them, a reductive cadence ironically placed in a cosmic setting. "The sun touched the sea, and for thirty seconds every detail of the distant man-of-war was outlined in black against the flame. But, for the life of him, Jonsen could think of nothing but that house in quiet Lübeck, with the green porcelain stove" (Hughes, *A High Wind in Jamaica*, Chapter 8).

We have seen, in a cadence from *Vanity Fair*, that Thackeray's syntax, the very shape of his sentences, induces a sense of finality. In most cadences something of the effect of Thackeray's syntax and dictional evocation occurs. Periodicity, unusual length, and the series are especially characteristic of last sentences. A cadence from Book III, Chapter 5 of Jane Austen's *Emma* confirms the appropriateness of periodicity in an ending. "That he might not be irritated into an absolute fever, by the fire which Mr. Woodhouse's tender habits required almost every evening throughout the year, he soon afterwards took a hasty leave, and walked home to the coolness and solitude of Donwell Abbey." It is unusual for Jane Austen to delay her main subject and verb until twenty-five words of subordinate clause have occurred. The main clause carries with it an especially emphatic finality because its audience has had to wait for it and attend to it, an effect that is seen also by the frequent use in the nineteenth century of the periodic sentence at the end of public addresses. The finality which a series is capable of evoking is confirmed by a cadence from Chapter XXVII of Trollope's *Barchester Towers*: "Mr. Slope said but little on the subject of Sabbath schools, but he made his adieu, and betook himself home with a sad heart, troubled mind, and uneasy conscience."

Something of the possibilities of suggesting finality by means of unusual length, or the illusion of unusual length, is contained in this cadence from Conrad's *Victory*. "The girl he had come across, of whom he had possessed himself, to whose presence he was not yet accustomed, with whom he did not yet know how to live; that human being so near and still so strange, gave him a greater sense of his own reality than he had ever known in all his life" (III, iii).

Similarly, not many of Jane Austen's sentences are so long as this one, and few of her sentences achieve such a solid quality of summary:

To know that she had the power of revealing what would so exceedingly astonish Jane, and must, at the same time, so highly gratify whatever of her own vanity she had not yet been able to reason away, was such a temptation to openness as nothing could have conquered, but the state of indecision in which she remained, as to the extent of what she should communicate; and her fear, if she once entered on the subject, of being hurried into repeating something of Bingley, which might only grieve her sister farther. (*Pride and Prejudice*, II, 15)

Such chapter endings, whether they seem explicitly to summarize or not, suggest rhythmically the tone of assessment when contrasted with the "he saids" and "she saids" of the chapter as a whole.

Not only may a sense of conclusion be induced by a final sentence or a group of final sentences somewhat longer than the stylistic norm, but it can be induced by an unusually short last sentence. Against the Jamesian norm, the nervous, almost telegraphic brevity of these syntactic units in *The Wings of the Dove* contrasts forcibly. "She hadn't lost the old clue; there were connexions she remembered, addresses she could try; so the thing was to begin. She wrote on the spot" (Book III, Chapter II). Or again: "So Milly was successfully deceived" (Book VI, Chapter IV). And again: "So far she was good for what he wanted" (Book VIII, Chapter II).

The syntax of a last sentence may induce a sense of finality by a kind of incantatory repetition. The effect, in prose, is analogous to the poetic effect of Housman's "And ah! 'tis true, 'tis true" or Frost's "And miles to go before I sleep,/ And miles to go before I sleep." Chapter 9 of Huxley's *Antic Hay* ends, "How smooth they were, how soft and warm and how secret under the sleeves. And all her body was as smooth and warm, was as soft and secret, still more secret beneath the pink folds. Like a warm serpent hidden away, secretly, secretly." Dickens is a consummate master of the repetitive cadence, as these examples from *Bleak House* demonstrate.

"Do they look like that sort of thing?" said Ada, coming laughingly behind me, and clasping me merrily round the waist. "O, yes, indeed they do, Dame Durden! They look very, very like that sort of thing! O, very like it indeed, my dear!" (Chapter XVII)

Dead, your Majesty. Dead, my lords and gentlemen. Dead, Right Reverends and Wrong Reverends of every order. Dead, men and women, born with Heavenly compassion in your hearts. And dying thus around us every day. (Chapter XLVII)

Lastly, many of the section endings in Faulkner's *As I Lay Dying* are such incantatory repetitions. " 'Jewel,' I say, 'do you know that Addie Bundren is going to die? Addie Bundren is going to die?' " (Modern Library Edition, p. 366). "And then I knew that I knew. I knew that as plain on that day as I knew about Dewey Dell on that day" (p. 435). "I have not been on the train, but Darl has been on the train. Darl. Darl is my brother. Darl. Darl" (p. 526). " 'Yes yes yes yes yes yes yes yes' " (p. 527).

Up to this point some categories have been devised and some forms isolated at the risk of creating two impressions which it is necessary to qualify. First, the very act of classification seems to suggest that each kind of cadence is exclusive of every other kind, whereas we have seen that, in practice, any given ending is likely to contain several different cadence techniques operating simultaneously. Secondly, the discussion has unavoidably suggested that the concept of cadence refers to an area of formal manipulation which can be defined, described, and extracted, for purposes of examination, from the chapter in which it operates. But it is obviously impossible to tell when an ending begins. Those sentences quoted as examples of last sentences are preceded by penultimate sentences which, even though they may contribute rather little to a sense of conclusion, anticipate the last sentence and thus are inescapably a part of the ending. And so it goes. The ending of a chapter is implicit in its beginning, which is not to say that the formal devices of its conclusion do not exist.

There remains, however, a final logical problem. It is illustrated by the following passage from *Persuasion*.

Frederick Wentworth had used such words, or something like them, but without an idea that they would be carried round to her. He had thought her wretchedly altered, and, in the first moment of appeal, had spoken as he felt. He had not forgiven Anne Elliot. She had used him ill; deserted and disappointed him; and worse, she had shown a feebleness of character in doing so, which his own decided, confident temper could not endure. She had given him up to oblige others. It had been the effect of over-persuasion. It had been weakness and timidity. (Oxford Edition, p. 61)

It is an extraordinarily shaped paragraph, its parallel series of charges rising in their emotional intensity, its last two parallel sentences summarizing both the paragraph and the whole series of events prior to the beginning of the novel to which they refer. The end of the paragraph displays the rhythmic, epigrammatic, summary qualities that Jane Austen's chapter endings often do. But the paragraph does not occur at the end of a chapter; it occurs in the middle of one. The presence of the devices which can suggest finality at various midpoints in a work is not peculiar to fiction, of course, but characteristic of any time art.

In its position at the end of a Bach chorale, a particular seventh, followed by a particular tonic, is a cadence to the theoretician, and the harmonic progression is felt to be an ending by the most un-theoretic listener. But the same seventh followed by the same tonic in mid-work does not suggest a conclusion at all.

What happens in a chapter which ends with a cadence (and again not all chapters do) is that the configuration of the chapter as a whole is managed in such a way as to make it possible to enclose the chapter at one level, at least, of its operation. A triangle, that basic gestalt figure, engages the observer's perception at one level, a two-dimensional spatial level. A chapter, of even the simplest fiction, engages the reader's imagination at a dozen levels—of time, of space, of syntax, of thematic development, of irony. A novelist for whom the cadence is a useful device deploys the materials of his chapter so that a convincing enclosure is possible at one or more levels, effects his enclosure by means of those devices which suggest finality although most of those devices may appear elsewhere in the chapter, and at the same time he permits certain other dimensions of his fiction to remain open and unenclosed. Subtle and elusive as the technique of the cadence may be, few other esthetic phenomena can evoke such nearly unanimous gratification—a nearly universal feeling among readers at the primary level where the work is directly experienced—that the artist, by means of his craft, has made an ending which does not end the work.

4
Open Ends

WHEN examining the techniques of fictional enclosure, it is easy to ignore what cannot, finally, be ignored: that many chapters simply are not, in a formal sense, enclosed. No identifiable devices which could be called cadence appear at the end of such chapters. The chapter simply stops, as if the convention of dividing long prose fictions into chapters were only a mechanical exigency, an annoying habit of the typesetter, an irrelevant expectation by the reader, a meaningless convention against which the novelist were obliged to oppose himself by making the units of his narrative, despite the fact that they physically end, seem not to end at all. The convention of ending may invite the possibility of violating it and so creating a passage of shock, surprise, and power.

Chapter XXIII of Book VI of *The Awkward Age*, for example, ends in this manner:

She was instantly gone, on which Mrs. Brook had more attention for her son. This, after an instant, as she approached the sofa and raised her eyes from the little table beside it, came straight out. "Where in the world is that five-pound note?"

Harold looked vacantly about him. "What five-pound note?"

So ends not only the chapter but an entire book of Henry James's novel.

Harold is one of those precocious and vicious children who turn up from time to time in James. He steals from his mother at other times in the novel, though elsewhere he ac-

knowledges the theft. Here the reader must assume that
Harold has committed the theft. James nowhere said that he
does, but for the reader not to assume Harold guilty is surely
to make nonsense of the passage. The reader also must make
what he can of the theft. Is it a clever gesture intended by
Harold to demonstrate a kind of superiority over his mother?
Is it an act so essentially neurotic as to defy motivational
analysis? Is it a kind of childlike revenge for one of those
characteristically Jamesian scenes where the adults go on with
their adult talk, oblivious of the perceptive but apparently innocent child nearby? Is it less an act significant in itself than
a judgment of Mrs. Brook? Mrs. Brook is certainly judged in
the next-to-last paragraph, where her "more attention to her
son" turns out to be concern for a stolen bill. Is the theft an
expression of the quintessence of Harold, or is it an expression of a different Harold, a culmination? With a summary
sentence, James could have settled his chapter with both certainty and finality, perhaps something about Harold's satisfaction, or his mother's obtuseness, or the insight of either
of them into what is going on. But such a sentence James
will not provide.

In the case of a chapter that ends with a setting sun, one
can be reasonably sure of the author's intention as the characters fade away into the cosmic twilight; readers will respond
to the ending in rather similar ways. Such an ending as
James's is baffling by comparison. Nevertheless, it is possible,
however tentatively, to find some esthetic principles behind
the efforts of writers of fiction to subvert the very chapter
divisions which they feel compelled to make, to protest
against these breaks in continuity, and to ignore the conventions which the making of chapters seems to demand.

Generally, these esthetic principles are of two kinds, the

comic and the mimetic. That is, the reader's expectations that the chapter will end are violated in such a way as to produce an effect that is ludicrous or satiric, witty or grotesque. On the other hand, the abruptness of the chapter ending and the disregard for the conventions of seeming to end may be a calculated attempt to render fictionally some aspect of the way in which the novelist views the world at large—a view, perhaps, of the operation of the mind or of the metaphysical continuity of the world or of the social disintegration which the writer sees in experience, projected into the images of the novel. All of these are views which may make the tradition of cadence, with its tranquil enclosure and its suggestion of philosophical certainty, unusable. These two categories are not mutually exclusive. A novelist may achieve comic effects by means of his formal manipulations at the same time that he is attempting to get his imaginative vision down on paper as accurately, and if need be as unconventionally, as possible.

Erich Auerbach's *Mimesis* provides a rich, panoramic discussion of comic and mimetic possibilities and their interrelation. Near the beginning of his book Auerbach contrasted two polar styles that stand at the very origins of Western literature, the Homeric and the biblical. The Homeric, he wrote, is characterized by "fully externalized description, uniform illumination, uninterrupted connection, free expression, all events in the foreground, displaying unmistakable meanings, few elements of historical development and of psychological perspective." Biblical style, on the other hand, is characterized by "certain parts brought into high relief, others left obscure, abruptness, suggestive influence of the unexpressed, 'background' quality, multiplicity of meanings and the need for interpretation, universal-historical claims, development of the concept of the historically becoming, and preoccupation with the problematic." [1] However distant the story of Abraham and Isaac may be from James's Mrs. Brook and Harold, it is altogether plausible to see a kinship between the two in their mutual occupation of the same stylistic areas. For we need know no more of Mrs. Brook and Harold than the chapter ending to see James in pursuit of a reality that shares many features with the reality imitated by the author of Abraham and Isaac—complicated, partly hidden, abrupt and discontinuous, ambiguous, and problematic.

At the other end of *Mimesis*, Auerbach summarized what seemed to him distinctive in the realistic novel after World War I: "multipersonal representation of consciousness, time strata, disintegration of the continuity of exterior events, shifting of the narrative viewpoint" (p. 546), suggesting that the ambiguous, difficult, problematic character of much of twentieth-century literature is a continuation of that ancient mimetic mode which Auerbach finds as early as the Bible. Between the two historical extremes of Petronius and Rabelais, Cervantes and Moliere make clear that such a mimetic mode gives form to some of the most richly comic imaginations in Western literature.

James's ending in *The Awkward Age* is to some extent a result of a highly specialized mimetic mode, a result of the view, adopted for purposes of the novel, in which only so much of experience matters as can be rendered scenically. It is a result of a search for formal expression of certain shallow social relations and certain rather petty states of mind. But James's ending is also highly comic. Mrs. Brook is not only ridiculously ineffectual, gulled as she is by a small boy; she is

[1] *Mimesis: The Representation of Reality in Western Literature*, trans. Willard R. Trask (Princeton: Princeton University Press, 1953), p. 23.

doubly ineffectual because of the very form of the chapter.
She is forever paralyzed, unable to find "that five-pound note,"
since James will not let the chapter continue. In a similar way,
Harold, his guile written on his vacant look, is forever frozen
on page 273 with his question "What five-pound note?" unanswered.

A poetic prototype for the comic possibilities in manipulat-
ing the narrative break occurs in *The Rape of the Lock*, by
Alexander Pope.

> Uncurl'd it hangs, the fatal Sheers demands;
> And tempts once more thy sacrilegious Hands.
> Oh Hadst thou, Cruel! been content to seize
> Hairs less in sight, or any Hairs but these!
>
> ### Canto V
>
> She said: . . .

Nothing could diminish the gravity of Belinda's speech more
than the physical detachment of "She said." Such a delayed
attribution has its epic analogues—the long speech in Homer
or Virgil, followed by white space, followed by something
like "Thus spoke the noble Aeneas." But Pope's "She said"
lacks the elevation of epic diction and the summary quality
of the epic attribution. It is the barest, simplest attribution
possible in English, and thus it contributes to the mockery of
epic pretensions which is the spirit of the poem. It is not only
its flatness but its position that makes "She said" comic, since
the phrase cannot carry with it, as the epic attribution can,
justification for that momentous pause which the reader must
make. A large part of the comic force of the passage, in other
words, is not directed toward Belinda but toward Pope.

It is the nature of the mock epic in the eighteenth century
that it seems to mistake the trivial for the important, that it
seems to compare equally the death of husbands and lap dogs,

that it plays with the possibility that the poet is as ludicrous as his subjects are, while encouraging us to see that all of the self-mockery of the poet *is* a game, that he is in fact extraordinarily perceptive.

In the passage cited, it is as if what must be enclosed within Canto IV cannot be managed there so it hangs out, dangles into Canto V—as if a carpenter, building two houses, finished the first only to find some windows left over and so put them gratuitously onto the second house. It is a pretense of formal ineptitude, all the more ironic because of Pope's cool brilliance in the management of his formal structures.

Trollope, in *Barchester Towers*, ended Chapter III with something rather like Pope's comic use of the narrative division. "Mr. Slope, however, on his first introduction must not be brought before the public at the tail of a chapter." Of course, if Mr. Slope must not be introduced until the next chapter, then there is little point in bringing up his name in the present chapter. Introducing him at the end of the chapter does whet the reader's appetite, but it seems to do so at the expense of the narrator's appearance of control. As with Pope, the comedy is directed both toward the subject matter —an undercutting of Slope even before he is properly introduced—and toward the manner of narration, since Trollope's deployment of his narrative takes place in a work which we judge to be carefully and precisely made yet which seems, for the moment, to display a naive ineptitude in the adjustment of subject matter to physical form.

A classic, as well as the most outrageously comic, example of such technical play with the chapter break occurs in *Don Quixote*. "But the unfortunate thing," Cervantes began one of his last paragraphs, "is that the author of this history left the battle in suspense at this critical point, with the excuse that he could find no more records of Don Quixote's exploits than those related here." The author, however, persuaded that further records exist, has found more and promises to relate their contents as the chapter ends. The next chapter begins with Don Quixote and the Basque frozen, their swords in the air. And for four pages, Cervantes described his quest for the records, his motives for the search, and the veracity of Benengeli. At last the narrative resumes: "The trenchant swords of the two valorous and furious combatants, brandished aloft, seemed to threaten the heavens, and earth, and the pit of hell, such was their courageous aspect" (Cohen translation, Penguin Edition, pp. 74–78). Cervantes' formal manipulations here permit him to mock the convention of cliffhanging chapter endings and the conventional management of suspense. They enable him to induce in the reader a comic distance at a potentially bloody point in the narrative. And they enable him to assert the fictive truth of his novel at the same time that he denies its literal truth by discrediting Benengeli.

Alice in Wonderland suggests still another way in which the chapter break can become a comic device. "Alice watched the White Rabbit as he fumbled over the list, feeling very curious to see what the next witness would be like, '—for they haven't got much evidence *yet*,' she said to herself. Imagine her surprise, when the White Rabbit read out, at the top of his shrill little voice the name 'Alice!' " Chapter XII begins, after a typographical space break, with " 'Here!' cried Alice, quite forgetting."

In his book entitled *Laughter*, Bergson constructed an elaborate theory of the comic on the assertion, first, that laughter is only possible with human objects—not, for example, with landscapes—and that we laugh when we perceive human objects, which we know to be intelligent, flexible, and adaptive, behaving as if they were machines, rigid, repetitive, and sub-intelligent. For Bergson, the common basis of things comic is the discovery of "something mechanical encrusted on the living." [2] In Lewis Carroll, the narration is a living thing, intelligent and intelligible, related to us by a human being, and its transition from chapter to chapter is immediate and continuous. Yet it is broken, as if by the random and unaccountable action of an erratic linotype machine—a particularly apt example of Bergsonian comedy.

If the purposes for avoiding the appearance of an ending at the points where the parts of a novel physically end are comic and mimetic, then Sterne, in *Tristram Shandy*, accomplished a remarkable fusion of the two. The raw materials of life are so formally intractable for Tristram that the conventions of chapter construction violate Sterne's mimetic obligations; for Sterne to transfer the raw materials of experience onto the page is for him to make chapters that inevitably collide with the reader's formal expectations. And this collision is comic. "A sudden impulse," wrote Sterne in his chapter on chapters, "comes across me—drop the curtain, Shandy—I drop it— Strike a line here across the paper, Tristram—I strike it—and hey for a new chapter" (IV, 10). The conventional wisdom regarding the making of chapters, Sterne continued, is "a story of a roasted horse." Do chapters "relieve the mind"? Do they "assist—or impose upon the imagination"? These are "cold conceits, enough to extinguish the fire which roasted" the horse. Indeed, in order to understand such matters, one had better read Longinus, and if one does not understand him, then one can read him again. "How my father went on, in my opinion," wrote Sterne, rather Tristram, some pages later, "deserves a chapter to itself." The next chapter begins:

[2] *Comedy: An Essay On Comedy by George Meredith and Laughter by Henri Bergson*, ed. Wylie Sypher (Garden City, N.Y.: Doubleday, 1956).

"—And a chapter it shall have, and a devil of a one too—so look to yourselves" (V, 3).

Part of Sterne's bag of tricks is to end a chapter now and then with a conventional, indeed a virtuoso, cadence. "My uncle Toby never felt the consciousness of his existence with more complacency than what the corporal's, and his own reflections, made him do at that moment; he lighted his pipe, Yorick drew his chair closer to the table—Trim snuffed the candle—my father stirred the fire—took up the book—coughed twice, and began" (V, 30). Such a cadence is an image of order which Sterne rarely permitted himself, with its unanimity of purpose in Tristram, Yorick, Trim, and Walter Shandy, with its clarity of beginning, and with its perfect conventionality of time sequence. A more characteristically Shandean ending is this one: ". . . —for as he opened his mouth to begin the next sentence, Chapter 15 In popped Corporal Trim with Stevinus" (II, 14–15).

Other comic novels are inventive or witty, suggesting that comic fiction often involves a heightening of the comedy latent in experience itself. Sterne's novel, on the other hand, suggests the possibility that fiction is most comic when it is least arranged. Simply by seeming to attempt an earnest, truthful imitation of experience, the novelist inevitably writes comedy. In a sense, Sterne's position is misleading; he contrived and arranged as much as any comic novelist. But in another sense, Sterne was perfectly right. His time scheme and his vision of the inner life were undertaken with a sense of mimetic fidelity; insofar as they succeed mimetically, they are funny, and his virtuoso endings are functions of this double purpose.

With a slightly different variety of the comic open end, Thomas Love Peacock ended Chapter V of *Crotchet Castle* with a speech by Lady Clarinda. "So you will see, some morning, that my novel is 'the most popular production of the day.' This is Mr. Puffall's favorite phrase. He makes the newspapers say it of everything he publishes. But 'the day,' you know, is a very convenient phrase; it allows of three hundred and sixty-five 'most popular productions' in a year. And in leap year one more." It is difficult to say whether Lady Clarinda possesses a penetratingly comic, indeed a Shandean, imagination, or whether she is an idiot. In any case, the last sentence is so petty, so irrelevant in all but the technical sense in which it is true, so anticlimactic that it mocks the convention of the cadence, which one expects to be, if not resounding, at least reasonably climactic. And thus the ending, by diminishing its own function as ending, adds to the comic force of Peacock's novel.

Mimetically, the novelist's technical manipulations at the point where his chapters come together is a result of the conflicting claims of continuity and discontinuity. These conflicting claims find a remarkable treatment in *The Counterfeiters*, by André Gide. Midway through *The Counterfeiters* Edouard pays his second visit to the old musician La Pérouse. The scene is heavy with ironic comparisons between life and art: La Pérouse's marriage is barely tolerable; the peace in his life comes from the contemplation of art; yet even Beethoven will allow him no tranquility but will write an entry for the trombones that destroys his serenity. "Have you observed," complains La Pérouse,

that the whole effect of modern music is to make bearable, and even agreeable, certain harmonies which we used to consider discords?"

"Exactly," I rejoined. "Everything must finally resolve into— be reduced to harmony."

"Harmony!" he repeated, shrugging his shoulders. "All that I can see in it is familiarization with evil—with sin. Sensibility is blunted; purity is tarnished; reactions are less vivid; one tolerates; one accepts. . . ."

"But you don't pretend to restrict music to the mere expression of serenity, do you? In that case, a single chord would suffice—a perfect and continuous chord."

He took both my hands in his, and in a burst of ecstasy, his eyes rapt in adoration, he repeated several times over:

"A perfect and continuous chord; yes, yes; a perfect and continuous chord. . . . But our whole universe is a prey to discord," he added sadly.

I took my leave. He accompanied me to the door and as he embraced me, murmured again:

"Oh! How long shall we have to wait for the resolution of the chord?" (Modern Library Edition, p. 165)

In his *Journal of "The Counterfeiters"* Gide wrote: "This novel will end sharply, not through exhaustion of the subject, which must give the impression of inexhaustibility, but on the contrary through its expansion and by a sort of blurring of its outline. It must not be neatly rounded off, but rather disperse, disintegrate" (p. 449). Here the problems of continuity and resolution, conclusion and "disintegration," life and art, are given a kind of definitive statement. In the two passages, taken together, there is a remarkable complementary breadth. The tension between continuity and resolution is felt emotionally and intellectually, with spontaneity and detachment, as an abstract philosophical problem and as an intimate question of fictional craft. The subject, Gide wrote, "must give the impression of inexhaustibility." In different ways, all fictional subjects do just this.

Although a Chinese vase or a geometric painting by Mondrian may seem evocative of nothing beyond its own limits, paintings by Brueghel such as "The Fight Between Carnival and Lent" or "Dance of the Bride," rich as they are, suggest an even wider scene than they portray. No one assumes, in looking at such a painting by Brueghel, that all of the rustics visible on the day in which he painted his picture are captured within his frame. Part of the effect of such a painting must be the suggestion that the scene would have continued if the frame were larger, that there is an infinite number of little fat Dutchmen available to Brueghel, only a small portion of whom could be squeezed within his frame. That Brueghel should suggest such continuity where a Chinese vase does not makes Brueghel especially analogous to the novelist. For among all of the novelist's commitments, one which he cannot escape is his obligation to the surface of life. No one expects to find amplitude of physical detail and reality of surface in, say, Lucian's *True History* or Bunyan's *Pilgrim's Progress*. But the novel since Defoe can almost be defined by its attempt to contain or at least refract the empirical data of ordinary experience.

Even in Virginia Woolf's work, time can be suspended but sensations cannot. Those solid blocks of materialistic detail which she protested in Bennett may be absent from her own fiction, but few writers convey a sense of the landscape of London, the experience of the sea, and the look of certain people more forcefully than Virginia Woolf.

Fiction, even at its most anti-realistic, is capable of imitating the passage of ordinary experience in a way that most other art forms are not. At its most realistic, fiction can come remarkably close to what seems like unmediated scene, transcript, or literary photography without forfeiting its claim to be art. When fiction tends to pursue a nearly total illusion of reality, abruptness of ending can become a positive virtue, suggesting, as it may, a minimal contrivance by the author. But in any fiction, including the least photographic, the bulk of the sensory detail must suggest continuity and inexhaustibility (except perhaps for those mystery novels in which every detail is related to a crime, the solution of which explains every detail and dispels all interest in the characters). The suggestion of continuity and inexhaustibility, which is almost unavoidable in an art so potentially close to the chaos of experience, is a quality which a writer may exploit if he wishes.

At its simplest level, the compulsion to continue results in a continuity between chapters rather like the comic fusions of Lewis Carroll and Sterne. Chapter XIII of *The Scarlet Letter* builds a large degree of emotional pressure in Hester, followed by a new sense of her poise and resolution. It would have been easy and natural to have ended the chapter with a solid, final sense of this newly gained self-possession. But Hawthorne forced a continuity upon what would have been, perhaps, too easy a unit, too destructive of the emotional flow which he wished his narrative to maintain.

In fine, Hester Prynne resolved to meet her former husband, and do what might be in her power for the rescue of the victim on whom he had so evidently set his gripe. The occasion was not long to seek. One afternoon, walking with Pearl in a retired part of the peninsula, she beheld the old physician, with a basket on one arm, and a staff in the other hand, stooping along the ground, in quest of roots and herbs to concoct his medicines withal.

Hawthorne's next chapter, "Hester and the Physician," begins:

Hester bade little Pearl run down to the margin of the water, and play with the shells and tangled seaweed, until she should have talked awhile with yonder gatherer of herbs. So the child flew away like a bird.

There is structural justification for a new chapter, as Hawthorne's title, "Hester and the Physician," suggests. But the narration is continuous—continuous, moreover, in such a way not only as to seem entirely serious but perhaps even to make the substance of the new chapter all the more urgent.

It is only when the novel as a whole is comic that the reader is predisposed to find the open ends of Sterne and Lewis Carroll comic.

But, what is more to the present point, Hawthorne's narration gives the impression of perfect control. Whatever the stylistic success of the passage quoted, Hawthorne is in charge, and the words do what he wanted them to do. James, Pope, and Sterne were probably greater craftsmen than Hawthorne. But in those comic examples cited, there is a carefully induced appearance of a lack of control—in James, with his ironic ignorance of what it all means; in Pope, with his apparent failure to get all of Canto IV said before Canto V begins; in Sterne, with his apparent inability to arrange the chaos of his imagination. Thus, the same formal movement is capable of carrying great comic force and of suggesting the immense pressure of the continuity in a deeply felt and quite serious narrative.

The possibility of abruptness in the scenic method was suggested earlier, specifically in the case of The Awkward Age, where the conventional rhetoric of narrative management is scrupulously abjured and where every effort contributes to an illusion of a chunk of life almost arbitrarily carved out of the interminable whole of experience. This is not to say that James, even at his most scenic, did not write cadences, for he often did. But James's fondness for scene, coupled with an intense interest in the surface of social interaction, worked against the thematic resolutions and the dramatic relaxations that traditional cadence often represents. Manners are presented not always in service of some larger purpose but, at times, for their own sake, as a legitimate object of interest. When such a display of manners occurs, in James's or in any other novels of manners, the abruptness of the unit is an understandable consequence.

The second chapter of Book II of Fitzgerald's *Tender is the Night,* for example, ends with this speech: " 'We wanted to warn you about getting burned the first day,' she continued cheerily, 'because *your* skin is important, but there seems to be so darn much formality on this beach that we didn't know whether you'd mind.' " There is more to Fitzgerald's chapter than manners alone, but it is toward the display of manners that the chapter directs its main effort. It is entirely appropriate that the chapter should conclude with an example of characteristic talk—fragmentary, inconclusive, but quintessentially illustrative of those qualities of manners and mind that Fitzgerald wished to illustrate.

Evelyn Waugh divided narrative so frequently that he seemed almost to be making a parody of novelistic structure. A *Handful of Dust* contains, as a subtitle for Chapter 2, "English Gothic—I"; this chapter is divided into four subsections; and the first subsection is divided eleven times by white space. The whole chapter suggests, for a moment, one of those endlessly divided outlines that school children are sometimes compelled to write. What Waugh's chapter seems to be is a collection of brilliant miniatures, none of which really ends, none of which really begins, all of which make a kind of progressive narrative sense only in their totality.

One such subsection, for example, begins this way: " 'I should have thought it was very nice to be called a tart,' John argued, 'and anyway it's a word Ben often uses about people.' " The section ends thus: " 'Hooray. Thunderclap went very well today. We jumped a big post and rails. She refused to first time but went like a bird after that.' 'Didn't you come off?' 'Yes, once. It wasn't Thunderclap's fault. I just opened my bloody legs and cut an arser.' " As with Fitzgerald, the section exists not so much to get somewhere as to display manners and shared states of mind, so that the very fragmentary abruptness of the scene reinforces the ironic detachment. There is something redeeming about a scene of stylish, shallow conversation that leads somewhere; we can be persuaded that the shallowness and silliness is only an interlude, that the characters really do have human substance which they assert from time to time. But when such a scene merely stops, we have no grounds for that assumption. And when a novel contains dozens of such scenes, the image which it presents of unredeemed foolishness is powerful and appalling.

A final example of the usefulness of abruptness when the substance of a chapter strives for a bizarre approximation of the surface of life occurs in Dos Passos' *Manhattan Transfer*. The title of Dos Passos' chapter, "Nickelodeon," suggests something of the harsh vulgarity of the contents. The chapter is deliberately discontinuous and fragmentary. Such a passage as this is a fair sample: "HELP WANTED MALE. That's more your speed you rummy. Addressers, first class penmen. . . . Lets me out. . . . Artist, attendant, Auto, Bicycle and Motorcycle repair shop. . . . He took out the back of an envelope and marked down the address. Bootblacks . . . Not yet. Boy; no I guess I aint a boy any more. Candystore, Canvassers, Carwashers, Dishwashers. EARN WHILE YOU LEARN." For a chapter whose whole substance is want ads, subway posters, popular songs, smells, and fragmentary conversation, the only esthetically satisfying ending must be one that is jarringly abrupt and quite unfinished.

"What time's it?" she asks a broadchested wise guy. "Time you an me was akwainted, sister. . . ." She shakes her head. Suddenly the music bursts into Auld Lang Syne. She breaks away from him and runs to the desk in a crowd of girls elbowing to turn in their dancechecks. "Say Anna," says a broadhipped blond girl, "did ye see that sap was dancing wid me? . . . He says to me the sap he says See you later an I says to him the sap I says see yez in hell foist . . . and then he says, Goily he says. . . ."

It is, of course, both a surface and a philosophical interpretation, a kind of literary photograph and at the same time an emblematic representation of the nature of the world, that Dos Passos offered by the shape of his ending.

Finally, very little in fiction is not contained in those two compendiums of how things can be done, *Tristram Shandy* and *Ulysses*. Significantly, each novel exploits the possibilities of both enclosure and openness. Something rather like the fragmented urban world of Dos Passos occurs in Joyce's "Wandering Rocks" episode, for example, and in the same novel some of the most graceful cadences in prose fiction appear. The open end is useful in a hundred ways, as Joyce and Sterne surely knew, and for that matter as Chaucer knew before them, because the convention of enclosure, elusive as that convention may be, is one of the most firmly established in fiction. No matter how many times a novelist may leave us in mid-air, the avoidance of enclosure is a formal manipulation which few readers can ever entirely adjust to. The open end is a formal shock, demanding of the reader an assimilation of the unexpected in a way that can challenge responses all the way from the reader's sober expectation of continuity to the reader's metaphysic. The open end is nearly as great a shock the tenth time it occurs in a novel as it is the first, partly because it engages the reader's most basic and universal pattern-making impulses. In a genre as ill-defined and flexible as the novel, shocks to our sense of formal propriety are rarely possible. If such a shock is possible where the reader expects a chapter to end, then the open end must surely be one of the most inexhaustibly rich of all the rhetorical possibilities available to the novelist.

5
Beginnings

THE UNIVERSAL advice given by manuals on how to write fiction is that the aspiring writer begin briskly, with a sentence both arresting in itself and suggestive of the tone of the whole novel. It is not bad advice if one reflects on some of the great beginnings of prose fiction. "Dear Father and Mother, I have great trouble, and some comfort, to acquaint you with" (Richardson, *Pamela*). "It is a truth universally acknowledged, that a single man in possession of a good fortune must be in want of a wife" (Jane Austen, *Pride and Prejudice*). "I wish either my father or my mother, or indeed both of them, as they were in duty both equally bound to it, had minded what they were about when they begot me" (*Tristram Shandy*). "'Now, what I want is, Facts. Teach these boys and girls nothing but Facts'" (Dickens, *Hard Times*). "It was a bright cold day in April, and the clocks were striking thirteen" (Orwell, *1984*). It is good advice, that is, until one reflects on how partial and how easy it is.

Conrad's *Heart of Darkness* begins: "The *Nellie*, a cruising yawl, swung to her anchor with a flutter of the sails, and was at rest." "Nellie" is a name almost embarrassingly benign, and Conrad's image suggests the beginning of a nautical idyll. *Wuthering Heights* begins: "I have just returned from a visit to my landlord—the solitary neighbour that I shall be troubled with. This is certainly a beautiful country!" Lockwood's tone suggests only the rather fussy conventionality of his own mind, quite the opposite of the main action of the novel. No one would say that *Heart of Darkness* should not begin deceptively, that it should seem to resist being told. And no one would say that the slightly nervous, slightly disapproving first sentence of *Wuthering Heights*, together with the bland raptures that follow it, is not just right as a beginning for the elaborate counterpoint that is to follow.

The point is that there are beginnings and beginnings. Not only can the novelist make use of many kinds of directness, but also he may find a special virtue in indirection, even in the appearance of seeming not to begin. Every fiction suggests to its creator the need for discovering the logic of its beginning. And such needs, in time, form a body of conventions by means of which a fiction may seem to begin. But just as with endings, the logic of a beginning may demand the avoidance of convention—an avoidance which becomes, in its own time, a new convention.

By ordinary logic it is a bit capricious to begin a novel anywhere. Even the birth of the hero is not really a beginning, as those Victorian novels which trace the hero's genealogy before the hero appears readily testify. Gide wrote, in *Journal of "The Counterfeiters"*: "Oddly enough, my novel is taking shape in reverse. I mean to say that I am constantly discovering that this or that which has happened previously ought to be included. Thus the chapters are not added one after the other at all; but they are continually pushing back the chapter I originally conceived as the first" (Modern Library Edition, p. 398). Just as in the case of cadence, the conventions of beginning, artificial enough in a sense, grow nevertheless out of processes of perception, the ways in which we begin to become interested in a subject or begin to notice that a figure is separable from a ground.

First sentences of novels can be devious or direct, and one can find justification, both in the structure of novels and in one's own initial acts of perception, for such different ways of beginning. First sentences of interior chapters, on the other hand, begin after our interest has been aroused, after the fiction is under way, and after the novelist has brought a previous unit either to a cadence or to an open end. The novelist here asks us to begin to be interested in a slightly different way in a new body of material which is intimately related to the previous unit but which is capable of forming, in time, a new gestalt.

The cadence from *Vanity Fair*, in which George marches away with his regiment, achieves a solid sense of finality by the interaction of a number of different rhetorical and substantive movements. After so conclusive an ending, beginning again is no casual affair. Here is how it is done: "Thus all the superior officers being summoned on duty elsewhere, Jos Sedley was left in command of the little colony at Brussels, with Amelia invalided, Isidor, his Belgian servant, and the *bonne*, who was maid-of-all-work for the establishment, as a garrison under him" (Chapter XXXI). Thackeray's new beginning is remarkably Hegelian, a synthesis of what has gone before, a thesis for what is to come. Thackeray began his chapter with *Thus*, suggesting that what has gone before, the cadence of the preceding chapter, is not really an end at all but a reason, a condition, for what happens in the chapter now beginning. The military references of the cadence continue in the beginning, both in the diction and in the series, which suggests a chain of command. If the military description of the cadence was a bit ironic, being slightly pompous and theatrical, it is doubly ironic in the beginning, where it is applied to domestic affairs. The beginning also effects a shift of interest in both character and place, from George to Jos Sedley, from parade to *establishment*, all without anything so obvious as a *meanwhile* or a *let us now turn to.* What happens in Thackeray's beginning, then, is a movement in which, by a perfectly defensible logic, a conclusion becomes not a conclusion. A continuity of tone and attitude is maintained with what has gone before; the continuity of our interest in Amelia is maintained. But in an almost surreptitious way, a new subject matter is introduced.

Elsewhere a cadence from *The Mayor of Casterbridge* was cited as being particularly final. Chapter 5 ends, "Henchard was not to be drawn again. Having said this, he sat down." It is no simple matter to begin a new chapter with our interest both in Henchard and the question he discusses —the responsibility for a crop of bad wheat—so successfully terminated. But, as in *Vanity Fair*, though in a totally different manner, an end becomes not an end. Hardy's next chapter begins in this way.

Now the group outside the window had within the last few minutes been reinforced by new arrivals, some of them respectable shopkeepers and their assistants, who had come out for a whiff of air after putting up the shutters for the night; some of them of a lower class. Distinct from either there appeared a stranger— a young man of remarkably pleasant aspect—who carried in his hand a carpet-bag of the smart floral pattern prevalent in such articles at that time.

The stranger's carpet-bag suggests his transience and justifies his first appearance as late as Chapter 6. His actions are mysterious but his manners ingratiating. He speaks with a "quaint and northerly" accent. And thus with a sense of intrigue we find ourselves propelled into a new chapter. Significantly, however, what particularly arrests the stranger's attention and prompts him to address a note to the Mayor are Henchard's last words in the preceding chapter: "But it can't be done." Ultimately we learn that "it" *can* be done. Already we suspect it, with the unusual response of the stranger to Henchard's categorical denial. Thus an ending, Henchard's peremptory remarks, is no ending at all but a prelude instead.

The movement from chapter ending to the chapter beginning that follows it in traditional fiction is not simply some kind of facile compromise between ideal continuity and the demands of the audience. Such endings and beginnings as those cited from Thackeray and Hardy achieve, not despite the typography of chapter division but with the aid of it, an impressive representation of continuity, even though continuity is observed from a different point of view from that in such densely introspective fiction as Dorothy Richardson's and Virginia Woolf's. The view of Thackeray and Hardy is one that recognizes the reality of endings, pays psychological and esthetic tribute to their finality, and then proceeds to transcend the endings with the ironic and paradoxical recognition that they are, in fact, beginnings.

Traditional fiction does not always present the interlocking beginnings and endings that one finds in the fiction of Thackeray and Hardy. A novelist may choose, for example, to inject an operative interval between chapters, a typographic pause during which an ending can resonate in the reader's mind in a way that no internal material can, tempering and predisposing the reader to understand the new beginning in a significantly different way.

The novelist may wish to use the distance between ending and beginning as a deliberate confusion, as a structural device participating in a general intent to delay synthesis, so that in a rapid, unmodulated shift from one subject to another the relationship between the two is impossible to see but all the more necessary to look for as the novel continues to unfold. Fitzgerald, for example, created an operative interval in the space between Chapters III and IV of *The Great Gatsby*.

Chapter III ends: "Every one suspects himself of at least one of the cardinal virtues, and this is mine: I am one of the few honest people that I have ever known." It is obvious that the beginning which follows such an ending need have no particularly close temporal or spatial connection with it; there need be no rigorous continuity of action or perpetuation of theme. Beginning almost anywhere, the new chapter will still be powerfully connected with what has gone before because Nick's last words, at once naive and sardonic and above all eminently credible, echo through the interval and modify what begins.

Chapter IV begins in this way: "On Sunday morning while church bells rang in the villages alongshore, the world and its mistress returned to Gatsby's house and twinkled hilariously on his lawn." The ironic juxtaposition of church bells and the gaudy meretriciousness of Gatsby's house take, for a background, the recollection that they are perceived by an honest mind. Thus Chapter IV begins not out of some inevitability of plot but rather out of the operative interval created by the previous ending.

As an example of the distant beginning for purposes of suspending synthesis, Joyce ended the "Telemachia" of *Ulysses* with this lush and evocative cadence: "He turned his face over a shoulder, rere regardant. Moving through the air high spars of a threemaster, her sails brailed up on the crosstrees, homing, upstream, silently moving, a silent ship." The chapter that follows introduces Bloom in a way that has nothing to do, apparently, with the time sequence of what has gone before, nothing to do with Stephen, nothing to do with the place where Stephen is located, nothing to do with the tone of the ship imagery: "Mr. Leopold Bloom ate with relish the inner organs of beasts and fowls. He liked thick giblet soup." Ultimately it will all come together. This one knows from rereading *Ulysses* and this one suspects on reading it the first time. Such a startlingly discontinuous beginning forces such an anticipation, but, more than that, it expresses the esthetic belief that order can be made out of the most startling discontinuities, in this case an introspective young intellectual, standing on a tower, picking his nose, and staring seaward, and a middle-aged, Jewish advertising canvasser on Eccles Street, preparing breakfast.

Abruptness of beginning can arise out of reasons rather less clear than those offered thus far, out of a generalized fondness for the fragmentary in fiction in ways that are analogous to an affinity for the open end. "I have a strong propensity in me to begin this chapter very nonsensically," wrote Sterne (Volume I, Chapter XXIII), and *Tristram Shandy* is a grand repository of nonsensical beginnings, many of which make the frailest connection or none at all with what has gone before and which provide no principle by which the new chapter can be organized. Chapter XIV of Volume VII, for example, begins, "—But she did not know I was under a vow not to shave my beard till I got to *Paris;*— yet I hate to make mysteries of nothing;—'tis the cold cautiousness of those little souls from which Lessius (*lib.* 13, *de moribus divinis,* cap. 24.) hath made his estimate." If to end conclusively is to falsify the mind of Tristram and the chaos of experience, then certainly it is as great a falsification to begin clearly.

It is not only fidelity to the chaos of the mind but fidelity to the chaos of society to which certain writers feel a special obligation. Evelyn Waugh began "English Gothic I," Section 3 of A *Handful of Dust* this way:

"Where's mummy gone?"

"London."

"Why?"

"Someone called Lady Cockpurse is giving a party."
"Is she nice?"
"Mummy thinks so. I don't."
"Why?"
"Because she looks like a monkey."

The passage that precedes this one gives no account of "mummy" which would prepare the reader for this exchange. The attribution of the speeches is omitted. And although everything is clear enough—who is speaking and what about —the effect is rather like entering a theater in the middle of a movie, disturbing in a not completely explicable way.

Abruptness of beginning, a justifiable eccentricity for Sterne, has become almost a commonplace for writers like Waugh, for many reasons—some common to both older and newer novelists, some uniquely modern. It is unmistakably true, for example, that both the endings and the beginnings of chapters in many nineteenth-century novels express the belief of the writer in the efficacy of social forms so that those satisfyingly decisive events—agreements, births, deaths, marriages—become at the same time means for marking off the chapters and ways of bodying forth the belief and trust of such novelists in the stability of character, in the basic viability of social conventions, in the intelligibility and purposefulness of experience. Consequently in newer novels in which a significant amount of interest is directed toward social coherence, twentieth-century skepticism has undercut the desirability of the poised and final ending and the poised and clearly delineated beginning as well. Abruptness of beginning can remind us of its expressive possibilities: seeming not to begin, like seeming not to end, is a way of saying something about the shape of the fictive world. Moreover, such abruptness can remind us of how chapters are made to seem to begin, not necessarily with the interlocking sequence used by Thackeray and

Hardy but by the use of many lesser conventions by means of which a new beginning is made to seem appropriate and believable. We are scarcely aware that such conventions exist until we become aware of their absence.

The most frequent set of conventions involves the making explicit of either time or place. "On the following Sunday," begins Chapter XXII of *Barchester Towers*, "Mr. Arabin was to read himself in at his new church." D. H. Lawrence began Chapter XIV of *The Rainbow*: "Maggie's people, the Schofields, lived in the large gardener's cottage, that was half a farm, behind Belcote Hall." Such a launching of the new action of the chapter in its own time and place can be invested with a large number of tonal effects. Dickens, for example, began Chapter VIII of *Bleak House* in a way that is both specific and general, that not only locates the action of the chapter but colors it with the benign openness of its narrator Esther: "It was interesting when I dressed before daylight, to peep out of window, where my candles were reflected in the black panes like two beacons, and, finding all beyond still enshrouded in the indistinctness of last night, to watch how it turned out when the day came on."

Beginnings, like endings, not only fix a point in a long fiction in space and time but also in the esthetic structure of the work itself. In Koestler's *Darkness at Noon*, the progressive, intensifying structure of the novel is made clear at the beginning of Chapter 13, for example: "The night was even worse. Rubachov could not sleep until dawn." In many novels a large part of our sense of an achieved esthetic structure comes from our perception of the characters' anticipations and realizations. What they guess will happen does or does not. What they hope for is fulfilled or frustrated. It is beginnings that can give this structural dimension of a novel its sharpest specificity. "As Mrs. Touchett had foretold, Isabel and Madame Merle were thrown much together during the illness of their host . . ." (James, *The Portrait of a Lady*, Chapter XIX).

Like endings, though in much diminished ways, beginnings can transcend the limits of the chapter, providing a context of psychological generalization or a frame of philosophical import or an aura of narratorial wisdom. Common to many of the beginnings in *Bleak House* are passages of great atmospheric and symbolic power: "Impassive, as behooves its high breeding, the Dedlock town house stares at the other houses in the street of dismal grandeur, and gives no outward sign of anything going wrong within" (Chapter LVI). Forster began Chapter XIV of *A Passage to India* aphoristically, in a way which reinforces our sense not only of the esthetic ground rules of his art but also the ironic poise of his narratorial voice: "Most of life is so dull that there is nothing to be said about it, and the books and talk that would describe it as interesting are obliged to exaggerate, in the hope of justifying their own existence."

Fiction ordinarily proceeds inferentially and inductively, drawing its conclusions from experience, or seeming to, rather than seeming to use experience to illustrate conclusions, so that when *Pride and Prejudice* begins with a "truth universally acknowledged" we read the phrase as an irony. For that reason, the philosophical beginning may seem pretentious and dogmatic in a way that the philosophical ending may not. Yet, for all its perils, the beginning which frames the chapter which follows it is one of the consistent conventions of the novel.

The conventions of the beginnings of chapters could be sketched at several times the length of the analysis begun here, but the construction of an exhaustive set of such conventions is not the point. The point, rather, is that such an analysis is possible, that a large, solid body of conventions exists, uncodified but quite accessible, which serves to link a new beginning with the established continuities of any novel.

The relation between a beginning and what is begun has been described occasionally here. It is a relation that eludes generalization, but another example can suggest, by way of summary, how important that relation is. All critics of *Emma* agree, if on nothing else, that a pivotal chapter of the novel is the excursion to Box Hill, in Volume 4, Chapter 7. Here any number of dramatic complications reach a climax, especially the humiliation, and consequently the full humanization, of Emma. It is an exceptionally intense chapter, at the end of which Emma confesses never having been "so agitated, mortified, grieved, at any circumstance in her life." Here is how the chapter begins:

They had a very fine day for Box Hill; and all the other outward circumstances of arrangement, accommodation, and punctuality, were in favour of a pleasant party. Mr. Weston directed the whole, officiating safely between Hartfield and the vicarage, and every body was in good time. Emma and Harriet went together; Miss Bates and her niece, with the Eltons; the gentlemen on horseback.

In thousands of novels, ominous chapters begin ominously; in Jane Austen's novel it is esthetically appropriate that a particularly intense episode should begin blandly. For the excursion to Box Hill to begin with threatening weather would be to dilute the moral failures which the chapter relates. But more than this, Jane Austen's beginning confirms again the value of chapters as structural devices. What the chapter accomplishes is the presentation of a partially enclosed, partially self-contained episode, deliberately begun and conclusively ended, which demonstrates a kind of failure and humiliation possible only when there is a clarity of purpose and a clarity of beginning. The crucial event of Emma's moral education must occur in a decent world of sunshine and order, "accommodation and punctuality," in which, in something called Chapter 7, a group of characters clearly *begin* to do something for which they have high hopes. To have sacrificed the conventions of chapters for the sake of an ideal of continuity would have been to have blurred the clarity of what the characters are beginning to do and consequently to have blurred the clarity of Emma's failure.

6
The Chapter as Symbol

ARTISTIC forms gather associations from the ways in which they are employed, as with the Aesopean fable, for perhaps the simplest example in narrative prose. In time such associations, the gradually accumulating sense of esthetic possibilities which attach to a form, become a shared and stylized way of meaning which is, in fact, symbolic. Fictional chapters are hardly so fixed in their conventionality that we can easily assign, as forms, the symbolic values which they carry; yet such a symbolic value is inevitably there, in the very shape of the chapter.

In a fragmentary, open-ended chapter, for example, any given novelist will put abruptness of ending to a somewhat different use. The fragment which makes up the chapter will be made out of a different implied whole, but the abstraction which we may call the open-ended chapter exists prior to any novelist's use of it. As an abstraction, it means something, with its inevitable components of surprise and frustration, its association with narrative perversity, the projection of contingency, and the suspension of valuation. It is possible that a novelist could wish to make an open-ended chapter which expresses, in the context of the whole work, tranquility, utter seriousness, poise, certainty, and satisfaction with the world of the novel. If this were done, the pre-existent value of the open-ended chapter would remain, and one could wonder why such an oddly distant form was chosen, judging it to be either a startlingly successful adaptation or a glorious ineptitude.

Imagine a chapter form which is basically episodic, which contains a unified complex of events involving a central character, but which opens out at its end into a cosmic cadence—a last paragraph devoted to the sunset, perhaps, or to an evocative description of the far horizon. Whoever the central character may be, whatever the nature of his episode, and whatever the total context of the novel, such a form carries a symbolic value which can be sketched in this way. To introduce cosmic imagery into a prose fiction is to frame the characters, to place them in some philosophical relation. To place the characters in relation to forces larger than the ordinary personal and social forces that govern their daily lives is to introduce a permanence into the narrative that contrasts with the transience of ordinary subject matter. It is to introduce an order of reality which transcends the realism of the narrative at large. It is to make something rather like a dramatized epigram, as if the intellectual symmetry of a maxim from La Rochefoucauld or a couplet from Pope had been expanded into a last paragraph.

What happens is a formal, rhetorical enclosure, not necessarily a thematic one. The introduction of the cosmic frame need not really resolve the tensions of a chapter. It may only induce a perspective toward them. No novel is wholly metaphysical; novels are immediate and realistic, and as they cease to be so, they cease to be novels, becoming expository prose instead. Thus, to introduce a larger-than-realistic element, a metaphor for man and the world, is to place the microcosm within the macrocosm (though, to admit a remarkable exception, *The Magic Mountain* does roughly the opposite). To make a chapter in this way is to make a symbol which presents, by its shape, a way of knowing and a way of feeling and which establishes the philosophical mode of the novel.

In fiction which is pretentious, the pretentiousness is likely to be evident in the way its chapters are made, for its chapters symbolize a degree of breadth which the substance of the chapters cannot support. The cosmic cadence is a stock device of bad fiction about the American West, but no amount of sunsets, tumbleweeds, and distant coyotes can convince an imaginative reader that a novel which is only a facile entertainment is really a story about man and the universe. It is the reader's expectation that the point toward which a chapter works will mirror the philosophical mode of the fiction that makes a failure to do so preposterous. It is this expectation that makes possible the ironies of Samuel Beckett's cadences, these from Chapter III of *Watt:*

And often he struck against the trunks of trees, and in the tangles of underwood caught his foot, and fell to the ground, on his back, on his face, on his side, or into a great clump of brambles, or of briars, or of thistles, or of nettles. But ever he picked himself up and unmurmuring went on, towards his habitation, until I saw him no more, but only the aspens. And from the hidden pavilions, his and mine, where by this time dinner was preparing, the issuing smokes by the wind were blown, now far apart, but now together, mingled to vanish.

Here in the breathless series, the throbbing rhythm, the archaic pretentiousness of such diction as *ever* and *habitation*, the imagery of hostile nature and mingling smoke, and the fussy details which distinguish *briars* from *brambles*, the whole tradition of providing a philosophical frame by means of a cadence is reduced to absurdity. But the absurdity would be impossible were it not for the fact that the chapter which broadens from the immediate to the cosmic conventionally projects a narrator who is ironic and detached, a narrator who has erected the formal means by which a kind of philosophical humility is symbolized—the formal means, moreover, by which the immediate and realistic is symbolically invested with depth, significance, and a universal resonance.

Let us examine another kind of chapter, frequent enough and obvious enough so that it exists as an option to any novelist who wishes to use it as a form. A chapter, for instance, develops at an almost exclusively scenic level a subject matter that is wholly social. No question is raised that reverberates beyond the immediate social group. No cause is introduced that originates outside the personal motives of the participants. Moral questions, let us say, are implied in the scene, but they are at all points implicit in the completely social action of the chapter. The chapter then works toward a temporary resolution which effectively summarizes the scene without seeming to end the book: a decision clearly made, an agreement shared among the participants, a course of action clearly undertaken.

As in the previous example, whatever the nature of the participants in the scene, whatever the total context of the novel, such a chapter form is symbolic, with a certain value attached to it as a form prior to its use by the novelist. What such a chapter symbolizes is a belief in the experiential possibility of what the chapter dramatically projects, a world in which social resolutions are, in fact, possible. Again, a novelist who believes that both in the created world of his novel and in the world of experience at large a marriage vow, for example, is a perilous, tentative, entirely uncertain undertaking, or a social reconciliation necessarily poses more ambiguities than certainties—such a novelist may bring his social chapter to a cadenced resolution. But it would be a choice of forms so apparently perverse that we should wonder why it was done. " 'I suppose I had better see Quiverful,' " says the chaplain at the end of a chapter of *Barchester Towers*. And the bishop replies, " 'I suppose you had.' " Whatever the merits of seeing Quiverful, whatever the ironic detachment of Trollope, one senses in the enclosure of his chapter an implicit approval of the social obligations that underlie the conversation and a wish to project a world in which such obligations can really be fulfilled.

To outline a third option, let us take a chapter which is concerned not so much with an externalized event, not so much with social interactions as with an individual state of mind, a treatment of conscience, or of motivation. Again let us imagine such a chapter working toward a conclusion which is as final and resolved as its position in mid-novel will permit. As with the previous forms, such a chapter, regardless of its contents, symbolizes a complex of feelings, a psychology, and a view of the world. Most chapters in twentieth-century fiction, when that fiction is highly internalized, are diffuse and inconclusive—so much so that it is generally difficult to say, after such a chapter is over, what it was about. When the opposite is the case, the shape of the chapter gives esthetic form to a view of personality in which mental processes have a discrete clarity and a view of the world in which the force of will is effectual.

C. P. Snow ended Chapter 2 of *The Search* in a way that is possible only when the mind is seen from a point of view that selects its rational and decisive moments rather than its blurred and irrational ones, and when the world is seen as being effectually changed by individual will: " 'I'm sorry.' I looked at him, embarrassed. 'I'm afraid I've decided already. I'm grateful to you for speaking—you know that? But, you see, I know what I want to do more than anything in the world; and I'm going to do it.' " As in the previous citations, a writer with, for example, Sterne's view of the world and the mind may construct a series of chapters that work toward decisive, resolved conclusions. But it is not clear how or why he should, and he would be aware certainly of the prior symbolic value which such chapters carry.

The first chapter of Frank Norris' naturalistic novel *The Pit* ends with a striking, if conventional, image of nature and the city—awesome, still, powerful, and animated so as to give the appearance of great potential hostility.

And this was her last impression of the evening. The lighted office buildings, the murk of rain, the haze of light in the heavens, and raised against it the pile of the Board of Trade Building, black, grave, monolithic, crouching on its foundations, like a monstrous sphinx with blind eyes, silent, grave—crouching there without a sound, without sign of life under the night and the drifting veil of rain.

To have arranged the chapter so that it works toward such a final point is to have summarized the esthetic premises of the chapter. The last paragraph is an enclosure; it makes the chapter seem to end, implying not that any of the substantial tensions of the chapter have been resolved but that the level at which the unit operates is conclusively established. The cadence does not seem to assert its juxtaposition of man and universe tentatively, experimentally, hypothetically, but dogmatically, like a fictional postulate of a doctrinaire philosophical system. Since fiction, naturalistic or not, must largely concern itself with change and development and modification, such a solid, static image of man and the universe is appropriate only at an end, as a philosophical summary which can put in perspective all of the blurry uncertainties of the chapter at large.

Any number of further characteristics modify and alter the capacity of a chapter's form to carry a symbolic weight.

The minor details of presentation and arrangement, for example, can influence quite powerfully our sense of a chapter's significance. George Eliot began each chapter of *Middlemarch* with an epigraph, some from earlier literature, frequently Shakespeare, some of her own composition. Mark Twain prefaced the chapters of *Pudd'nhead Wilson* with lines from Pudd'nhead Wilson's Calendar, a plausible combination of folk wisdom and learned irony. In both cases, the epigraphic beginning predisposes us to expect certain qualities of the chapter that is to follow, not just as a segment of the narrative but as a literary form with conventional and symbolic possibilities that allow it to be problematic or ironic or heavy with conceptual certainties.

Titles, similarly, are important in setting the symbolic limits of a chapter, and novelists, from Fielding to John Barth, who have chosen to use titles have often used them not simply as a name for the action to come but as a kind of lever by means of which the symbolic force of the chapter can be shifted. In a recent novel by Evan S. Connell, Jr., entitled *Mr. Bridge*, the chapters are discrete episodes with no temporal connection between them. They express the tight life of a Kansas City attorney in the 1930's, and their spare, narrow, self-enclosed form is highly appropriate to that style of life. Scarcely chapters at all, in the conventional sense, the individual segments of Connell's novel become, in their very form, highly symbolic of the constricted world they express. This symbolic value is reinforced by their titles. "Season's Greetings" is the title of one segment. It is an account—one page long—of Mr. Bridge's receiving a Christmas card from a senator who had never sent one to him before and who is up for reelection this year. The spare and formulaic phrase of the title interacts with the anecdote of the Christmas card, and the narrative unit is made to carry a heavy signification, the hollowness of the character's motives being shaped and contained within that titled and self-enclosed segment.

Arrangement into books or sections also modifies the symbolic values of the chapters which such arrangements contain. The meditative and narrative segments of Gissing's *Private Papers of Henry Ryecroft* are contained in sections named for the seasons. Thus any given segment carries with it a sense of its formal possibilities and a sense of its rhetorical signification as a form, simply by virtue of its occurrence within a section called "Spring" or "Winter."

Most of the great English novelists of the nineteenth century used section titles not only to shape the narrative but to give the individual chapters within the sections some sense of common formal value. The individual chapters of *Middlemarch*, in the section entitled "The Dead Hand," vary greatly from each other. But they all share some common qualities by means of which it is clear to the reader that they are, in common, the formal devices in which the dead hand of both the present and the past is given artistic coherence; to that extent those chapters carry certain subtle formal values which become symbolic.

In genres other than the novel, those forms carrying a clear symbolic signification are comparatively simple or comparatively old. The limerick, for example, is simple in its form, quite limited in its range, and old enough so that it has gathered a set of values that express something of its symbolic signification as a form. Heroic couplets can be invested with extraordinary virtuosity, but basically they, too, are simple in their form, and they are old enough so that it is impossible to use them now without some sense that they mean something as heroic couplets. The contemporary satiric poet Roy Campbell uses heroic couplets in order to exploit a traditional symbolic value that declares, in every line, that his poetry is spiritually not of our time at all. Rather, it seeks, atavistically, to measure human aberration against standards of reason, balance, and poise, as those standards are capable of being expressed by a form that found its fullest and most characteristic use in the eighteenth century.

As with verse forms, the fictional chapter is most clearly symbolic when it, too, is comparatively old or comparatively simple. Perhaps the most obvious instance of a fictional chapter which is both is the characteristic chapter of early picaresque fiction. It begins with arrival in a new place and attachment to a new way of surviving. The tensions of the chapter are basically physical—the picaro wishes to avoid hunger, pain, or fatigue. At a secondary level the tensions come from the psychological strategies the picaro employs to relieve his physical discomfort, and thus there are large amounts of ingenuity and naivete in the chapter, much humiliation and revenge. Beginning diffusely, the picaresque chapter ends specifically as it becomes increasingly clear in the progress of the chapter on what terms the antagonist must be bested. The chapter ends with a temporary victory in perilous circumstances so that the picaro must escape and begin the process anew in the next chapter.

In its classic form, as it appears in *Lazarillo de Tormes*, it is a beautifully economic unit with a concentration of force and a purity of structure rarely equaled in prose fiction since. It is, in fact, a unit so economical and concentrated that more recent novelists could not have duplicated its form exactly if they had wished. Characters in Smollett, for example, have much more to worry about than their bellies, and they have more games which they are driven to play than simply the games that would win them a loaf of bread. Still, there are countless novels that derive from the picaresque prototypes; in so doing they carry into their own times the typical actions of the picaresque novel, the typical character of the picaro, and the typical form (however swelled and complicated) of the picaresque chapter.

It is because that picaresque chapter carries so clear a symbolic charge that it is so endlessly adoptable and reusable. It is the narrative unit that best expresses social disintegration and rootlessness, constant stress, what we have come to call alienation. And so it is that the very shape of the chapter carries with it a symbolic value, just as surely as does the figure of the picaro himself.

The substance of a chapter, then—its pattern of action and above all its end, the minor details of its presentation, the traditional values that have been attached to its use—gives a chapter a symbolic weight that it would not carry if it were only an arbitrary segment of a total action. The conventions of chapters provide a mechanism by which the symbolic mode of a novel can be reasserted in a way that would be impossible in a continuous narration. Fielding generally arranged his chapters so as to assert, by means of their shape and their conclusions, their play upon the values of comparable forms, his social concerns, the typicality of his figures, and his tranquility with a world which he criticized but did not seek to change. When Dickens was sentimental, he contrived his chapters so that they worked toward his most melodramatic effects, so that each chapter restated anew the tenderness and pathos that the whole novel projects. D. H. Lawrence's Dark Gods were never so evident as at those points towards which his chapters work. In short, the conventions of chapter construction become conveyers of value in themselves, and they make possible an expression, in small, of the mode of the whole novels of which the chapters are a part.

III
Order

7
Parts and Wholes

————•◆•————

Probably there is no fuller catalog of ways of making sense than in the fiction of Samuel Beckett. They are all there: post-Cartesian philosophy, the scientific method, mathematics, psychoanalysis, gestalt psychology, institutional religion, transcendental metaphysics, time, history, myth, syntax, artistic form, and more. It is because none of these make sense to Beckett that the catalog is so comically exuberant and so complete. "As Watt told the beginning of his story," Beckett wrote, "not first, but second, so not fourth, but third, now he told its end. Two, one, four, three, that was the order in which Watt told his story. Heroic quatrains are not otherwise elaborated" (*Watt*, p. 214). Earlier in *Watt*, Beckett wrote: "To such an extent is this true, that one is sometimes tempted to wonder, with reference to two or three incidents related by Watt as separate and distinct, if they are not in reality the same incident, variously interpreted" (p. 78). So it goes, both in *Watt* and throughout Beckett's fiction, as the very nature of narrative is subjected to the same mock-serious analysis as are all of the other ways of arranging the data of one's world.

What Beckett's clowning with narrative order and the reality of the episode implies is that these have been powerful concerns, though perhaps implicit and half-conscious, of Western literature for some time. Insofar as the chapter is, or has been, as Beckett would prefer, an expressive narrative division and not simply an arbitrary embellishment, an in-

99

quiry into the function of chapters as parts of narrative wholes becomes potentially an access to the structure of novels and their ultimate meaning. It is a way of exploring, always a useful venture, certain objects of Beckett's burlesque.

In James's novella *The Beast in the Jungle*, the chapters are progressive in only a very minimal sense. If it is to be a story of the one man on earth to whom nothing was to happen, then nothing must happen. An impression of the passing of time is necessary to James's realization of his theme; the reader must perceive May Bartram, the central character's confidante, the woman whom he could love if he would, growing older and dying at last. As an exposition of the drama of lost chances and desperate inertia, a feeling of temporal progression is inevitable. Thus James's chapters are units of time in the sense that all chapters in all narratives are units of time and also in the special sense that the author's theme demands. But there is so little growth, so little movement, so little change in the novella that the function of the chapters as chronological units is not at all insisted upon. The first two chapters are roughly introductory, a striking climax occurs in the fourth chapter, another in the fifth, but no illumination occurs until the very end of the novella when the central character, John Marcher, understands at last who he is and what he might have been. While the work generates an impressive intensity and suspense, it is hardly because its chapters correspond to some classic symmetry of plot. Neither is the drama of James's novella analyzed into stages, aspects, or parts. Although the question of understanding is constantly before the reader, the chapters do not mark its degrees; we guess at May Bartram's understanding here and there, but John Marcher, until that final illumination, is monumentally, almost monotonously, self-oblivious.

James's notebooks help to illuminate what the chapters do

in *The Beast in the Jungle*. He wrote again and again of the slightness of his *données*, and not only his *données* but his intentions. In the germ of *The Beast in the Jungle* James saw "a very tiny *fantasie* probably." [1] What he planned to make into a story often turned into a "nouvelle"; what he planned to make into a nouvelle often became a novel. As he wrote he expanded, not so much the dramatic complexity of his fiction or its overt and explicit plot but rather its sheer development. "*Repetitive form*," wrote Kenneth Burke in *Counterstatement*:

is the consistent maintaining of a principle under new guises. It is a restatement of the same thing in different ways. . . . A succession of images, each of them regiving the same lyric mood; a character repeating his identity, his "number," under changing situations; the sustaining of an attitude, as in satire; . . . the rhyme scheme of *terza rima*—these are all aspects of repetitive form. By a varying number of details, the reader is led to feel more or less consciously the principle underlying them—he then requires that this principle be observed in the giving of further details. Repetitive form, the restatement of a theme by new details, is basic to any work of art, or to any other kind of orientation, for that matter. It is our only method of "talking on the subject." (p. 125)

James's chapters in *The Beast in the Jungle* are, in Burke's terms, repetitive forms. They mark stages, certainly, in the growing though covert understanding of May Bartram; they mark stages in the ironic understanding of the reader; they mark degrees of social complexity; and they mark degrees of emotional intensity. Primarily, however, the chapters are ways of showing the same act five times. Each chapter begins with an analytical introduction which is at the same time incisive

---

[1] *The Notebooks of Henry James*, ed. F. O. Matthiessen and K. B. Murdock (New York: Braziller, 1955), p. 311.

and extraordinarily obtuse, followed by a minutely rendered scene in which the two principals meet and converse and in which the central figure manipulates the symbol of the beast in the process of asking who he is and how he is to live, followed by the familiar fog, once again, of over-civilized and stifling analysis.

The idea of repetitive form in the novel brings to mind, perhaps, the recurrent, potentially monotonous situations of early picaresque. But a work so self-consciously formed and so highly sophisticated as *The Beast in the Jungle* was deliberately selected here to suggest that repetitive form, far from being a basic structure of crude and primitive fiction, is a pole toward which a great amount of fiction, of all degrees of complexity, tends. Chapters divide—indeed they make possible—repetitive forms in fiction as different as *Lazarillo de Tormes* and Peacock's *Nightmare Abbey*, Fielding's *Joseph Andrews* and Melville's *Confidence Man*, Mackenzie's *Man of Feeling* and Johnson's *Rasselas*, Joyce Cary's *Horse's Mouth* and Kafka's *Trial*.

The division of progressive form was discussed briefly in an earlier connection, specifically in the way in which chapter division can give a sense of clarity or urgency or thrust to the general progressive movement of a novel. Like repetitive form, progressive form is a pole toward which much fiction tends. Most novels, of course, express certain impulses in the direction of both poles. *Tristram Shandy*, propelled out of the changing mind of Tristram, still occupies itself with obsessions and recurrent motifs. *Middlemarch*, one of the most relentlessly progressive of novels, complements its progressive movement by a much-analyzed series of symbolic images as impressive in their repetitive power as the larger progressive movement. Despite the impossibility of writing fiction which is purely progressive or repetitive, however, one would not hesitate to locate the formal significance of *The Way of All Flesh* or *The Wings of the Dove* or *Sons and Lovers* in the growth and change which those novels express.

Kenneth Burke has analyzed progressive form of two subordinate kinds, and in both definitions one can see the usefulness, almost the necessity, of dividing the progression. "*Syllogistic progression,*" Burke wrote in *Counterstatement,* "is the form of a perfectly conducted argument, advancing step by step. It is the form of a mystery story, where everything falls together, as in a story of ratiocination by Poe. It is the form of a demonstration in Euclid. To go from A to E through stages B, C, and D is to obtain such form" (p. 124). On the other hand, "*Qualitative progression* is subtler. Instead of one incident in the plot preparing us for some other possible incident of plot (as Macbeth's murder of Duncan prepares us for the dying of Macbeth), the presence of one quality prepares us for the introduction of another (the grotesque seriousness of the murder scene preparing us for the grotesque buffoonery of the porter scene). . . . We are prepared less to demand a certain qualitative progression than to recognize its rightness after the event. We are put into a state of mind which another state of mind can appropriately follow" (p. 125). Why a novelist must segment a progressive whole into, as Burke put it, A, B, C, D, and E, or into incidents, qualities, and further incidents is a question that very soon becomes extra-literary, a question that can be answered, as shown in the first chapter, not in terms of the art of fiction so much as in terms of the mechanism of the mind.

By applying Burke's progressive-repetitive analysis to the question of the operation of chapters in entire novels, we can see that chapter division and chapter construction are expressive techniques that demonstrate, at every point, the conscious shaping of form according to the novelist's vision of his subject. The repetitive chapters of James are a realization of what James wished to do with his themes. To work in such a direction can hardly be surprising, in fact is in danger of becoming truistic, since it has become a commonplace to assert that style, form, and subject matter are really the same thing, that the old separation between what a work says and how it says it is indefensible. Such a position is necessary and defensible when dealing, say, with an ode by Keats. It perhaps is also true of a poem by Julia Moore, the Sweet Singer of Michigan, in which the banality of the technique and the banality of the subject matter make an indivisible whole. The premise of the unity of form and substance, however, is not a particularly useful critical principle when dealing with inferior poems of the later eighteenth century, which strive after sublimity with a handful of gestures derived from Milton and Pope as the wholly inadequate means to that sublimity.

Thus, there is a kind of literature in which the unity of its form and substance is a condition of its excellence. In another kind of literature, the unity of its style and substance is a condition of its inferiority. In a third kind of literature, through some lapse of taste or intelligence or technical insight, the style and the form—those things that can be analyzed out of a work under the rubric of technique—perform rather different and irreconcilable acts from what the substance of the work, insofar as it can be separated from the technique which presents it, seems to promise.

Of fiction, the technique of, let us say, Joyce's short story, "The Dead," *is* what the work says. It is perhaps just as evident that in much detective fiction the ultimate import of the fiction is slight, but the technique is perfectly adjusted to its substance. There is, however, a third area of fiction in which, as in pseudo-Miltonic poetry, the technique and the substance are not at all unified. And of those ways in which the technique of a novel can work against its thematic purposes, ineptness in the ordering of its chapters is a significant one.

Among the most popular novels ever written is Mrs. Susannah Rowson's *Charlotte Temple: A Tale of Truth*, first published in 1791 and reprinted in more than 160 editions in the century that followed in the United States alone. One tends to think of extraordinarily popular fiction as being technically proficient but imaginatively negligible. This is ironic since *Charlotte Temple* is an extreme example of the third group described above, an earnest novel the construction of which is gloriously inept. The first chapter reveals Montraville and Belcour, two officers, watching the neighborhood ladies returning from church. Montraville is immediately infatuated with Charlotte Temple and contrives to be introduced to her as the chapter ends. The second chapter, titled "Domestic Concerns," introduces Mr. Temple, a man of moderate means with a reputation for benevolence. He visits a retired officer in debtor's prison who is attended by a devoted daughter, and Temple is moved to tears. (One gathers only gradually that the second chapter has shifted the action many years into the past, before the birth of Charlotte.) In the third chapter, the Captain begins his own history, a tale full of betrayed innocence, in which he is jailed, his wife dies, his son is killed, and his daughter's honor is compromised. He continues his history in the following chapter. Temple determines to pay his debts for him, declares his love for the officer's daughter, and is alienated from his father, who wished him to marry the wealthy Miss Weatherby. In the fifth chapter, Miss Weatherby is described, the elder Temple proposes to her and is accepted, and the younger Temple marries the Captain's daughter with a much-reduced fortune. "Such were the parents of Charlotte Temple, who was the only pledge of their mutual love, and who, at the earnest entreaty of a particular friend, was permitted to finish the education her mother had begun at Madame Du Pont's school, where we first introduced her to the acquaintance of the reader." Something of the drift of the chapters that follow can be gathered from their titles: "An Intriguing Teacher," "Natural Sense of Propriety Inherent in the Female Bosom," "Domestic Pleasures Planned," "We Know Not What a Day May Bring Forth," and "When We Have Excited Curiosity, It Is But an Act of Good Nature To Gratify It."

The beginning of such an abysmally bad novel is summarized in this way in order to indicate how its structure goes wrong. The unity of the novel was evidently conceived as both a history of Charlotte Temple and an illustration of benevolence, temptation, and wronged innocence. But its construction was conceived by the chapter. The second chapter is on the model of Mackenzie's *Man of Feeling*, which is a repetitive structure, but it follows a first chapter which has begun as if to introduce a progressive structure. Some of the chapters are clearly episodes, some are units of a progressive development, and most are improvisations, indiscriminate in their inclusions. In some of the chapters, theme is allowed to predominate; as their titles indicate, they are exemplary. In others, action predominates—they are simply segments of an advancing plot. At every point at which the reader is likely to feel a particular lack of control—a confusion in time sequence, an awkward juxtaposition of the stylized and the verisimilar, a disregard for continuity—that point is likely to result from the fact that the novel was projected into chapters and that those chapters, borrowing their techniques of division and construction from a dozen different sources, will not come together.

At the opposite extreme, qualitatively, from Mrs. Rowson, one can examine Jane Austen's structural revisions in *Persuasion*. The transformations of the "cancelled" chapter have been perceptively analyzed by Walton Litz, who found that the revision of the original tenth chapter into two new chapters—the tenth and the eleventh—maintains Anne's point of view where the original two chapters had allowed it to lapse in favor of summary; that the revision disengages the dramatic climax of the revised material from the preceding climax, the proximity of which had tended to dilute its effect; that it decelerates the pace for a particularly significant effect; that it prepares the reader much more satisfactorily for the resolution in the last half of the novel; and that it intensifies the theme of isolation and the difficulty of communication.[2] In revising the chapters, Jane Austen made both substantive and verbal changes. But what is significant for the present discussion is that the scale, the construction, and the division of the chapters were changed also by way of making the part more precisely expressive of the whole. It would be difficult to find a purer example of the attempt to adjust form to idea and the wish to order the parts as precisely as possible within the whole.

In analyzing the forms of the plot, Norman Friedman spoke of the relation between short-term and long-term responses as a way of describing the effect of the plot upon the reader. In "the reform plot," for example, "after having been led to admire [the protagonist] at the beginning, we feel impatience and irritation when we begin seeing through his mask and then indignation and outrage when he continues to deceive others, and, finally, a sense of confirmed and righteous satisfaction when he makes the proper choice at last." In "the revelation plot, . . . we begin by feeling that every-

---

[2] A. Walton Litz, *Jane Austen: A Study of Her Artistic Development* (New York: Oxford, 1965), pp. 159–60.

thing is fine; our short-range fears develop and then are superseded by our long-range hopes." Or in *The Great Gatsby*, to choose a specific example, our long-range fears for the fragility of Gatsby's dream interact with our short-range hopes for the success of a good many of his individual ventures.[3] If chapters are units of progressive and repetitive forms, marking periods of time, units of space, degrees of intensity, stages of self-awareness, aspects of an analyzable whole, and so on, then chapters make convenient focal points for organizing and intensifying short-term and long-term responses. When we experience the ends of units in fiction we experience most deeply our short-term responses, but because we recognize these units as parts of larger wholes, we also feel most deeply at those points our long-term responses.

Until this point a minimal set of constructs have been provided by means of which chapters can be seen to clarify the movement of whole novels. Such formulas work best when applied to novels like Smollett's *Roderick Random* and Hasek's *Good Soldier Schweik*, Jane Austen's *Persuasion* and James's *Ambassadors*—works in which the formal design is consistently maintained and uniformly presented. The formulas apply less successfully to Dickens' *Pickwick Papers* and Dostoevsky's *Brothers Karamazov*—works which, in different ways, make a virtue out of an intentional, controlled inconsistency.

The relevance of the craft of chapter division, however, even to novels which seek to avoid formal uniformity, can be seen if one recalls those passages in *The Brothers Karamazov* that interrupt the progressive flow of the main actions. These interruptions are discourses, some of the most powerful in or out of prose fiction, and no one would deny their

[3] Norman Friedman, "Forms of the Plot," *Journal of General Education*, VIII (1955), 241–53.

intense relevance to the thematic progression of the novel. But they lie outside its regular rhythm of anticipation and fulfillment. Those discourses, however, are chapters, now and then pairs of chapters. Just as in a repetitive form where the conventions of chapters provide the frame for the item repeated, just as in a progressive form where the conventions of chapters provide the steps without which understanding of the progression is all but impossible, in a mixed and inconsistent form, the conventions of chapters provide the means by which the excursus, the interlude, or the interpolation can be set into the pattern of the whole novel.

Could "The Grand Inquisitor" be assimilated into a larger chapter or scattered throughout several other chapters of *The Brothers Karamazov*, rather than being, as it is, a single chapter given entirely to Ivan's vision and the conversation of Ivan and Alyosha regarding it? It is impossible to imagine the chapter in a different form. Passionate both in its conception and its narration, it must be whole, presented in such a way as to reinforce the image of its unity and integrity. At once being of the central characters and transcending them, it must be related, by certain conventional novelistic gestures, to what has gone before and what follows; yet it must be startlingly discontinuous with those intimate passions that make up the bulk of the novel. Both a part of the novel and a comment upon it, "The Grand Inquisitor" is a discourse among actions, a stasis among progressions, a continuation and an intensification of the novel's moral concerns, and a chapter to itself.

Chapter x of Book III in *Joseph Andrews* is entitled "A discourse between the poet and player; of no other use in this history, but to divert the reader." The reader of *Joseph Andrews* adjusts very quickly to a narrative order in which surprises, rapid shifts, violent contrasts, and interpolated mat-

ter occur. But at a superficial level, these surprises and contrasts fit rather well into a largely repetitive, neo-picaresque
form in which we expect to find Adams repeatedly gulled,
Fanny repeatedly imperiled, and Joseph repeatedly frustrated.
At a thematic level, these same surprises and contrasts make
sense as units of a repetitive form designed to illustrate the
benevolent ethic which historical critics have elucidated in
Fielding's work. But the discourse between the poet and the
player has nothing to do with Adams, Joseph, and Fanny, and
it has little to do with Fielding's ethic. It is admittedly presented as an interlude, an irrelevance. Thus it has become
one of the chapters of *Joseph Andrews* most worried over,
most attended to, most critically analyzed—all on the assumption that Fielding is being ironic, that he could not
mean it, that the chapter *is* "of use in this history."

Fielding's chapter can be shown to be relevant to the
design of the novel with only a moderate amount of ingenuity, but the point is not so much that this can be done as
that one feels the compulsion to do it. An irrelevant chapter,
even in a loosely organized work, is a challenge and a threat.
What is threatened is the image of control which the novel
presents and which one would like to believe in. What is
further threatened is the appearance of conviction which
underlies the act of dividing the narrative into parts. For
either these parts are intelligible in their ordered relation to
the whole or they are not. To confess that they are not is to
acknowledge esthetic ineptitude of the most damaging sort.
In serious fiction, the chapter as interlude is a device for
enlarging and complicating our idea of the progressive or
repetitive order of the whole work, an order to which the
interlude itself ultimately belongs. It is because it threatens
the order of the novel that the interlude can carry so much

force. Fielding's chapter, not a particularly interesting or distinguished chapter, can effect a revaluation of the shape and import of the whole novel, simply by Fielding's pretense that it does not belong.

Certain fiction, A *Portrait of the Artist as a Young Man* for example, is capable of impressing the reader with the inevitability of its chapters. That is, Joyce, however committed he may have been to the representation of continuity, believed, quite obviously, that Stephen is influenced in his development by the moralistic pressure of a Jesuit education and by his growing awareness of the power of beauty. Joyce believed, further, that these two influences are not the same, that they are separable, even though they may both be always present, and that it is artistically defensible to make them dominate separate sections of his fiction without sacrificing the radically developmental movement of the novel.

Other fiction, Thomas Hardy's for example, presents a divided whole in which division is no less necessary to understanding but in which it is less a conviction that shapes the chapters than a continually tentative and exploratory insight into the dramatic situations which the novel contains. Hardy suggested something like this when he wrote, "Like former productions of this pen, *Jude the Obscure* is simply an endeavour to give shape and coherence to a series of seemings, or personal impressions, the question of their consistency or their discordance, of their permanence or their transitoriness, being regarded as not of the first moment." [4] No one would maintain that the fitful liaison between Jude and Sue proceeds by means of inevitable units which are clearly analyzed parts of their whole emotional life. Yet those confrontations

[4] *Jude the Obscure*, Riverside Edition (Boston: Houghton Mifflin, 1965), p. 3.

and reconciliations that make up the chapters concerning Jude and Sue are necessary parts—necessary in their successive separateness.

Finally there is that kind of fiction which gives the appearance of pursuing disorder, pretending, with one degree of explicitness or another, that a chapter may belong to no larger whole at all, as happens explicitly in the chapter of *Joseph Andrews* "Of no other use in this history, but to divert the reader" and as happens implicitly again and again in Rabelais's *Gargantua* or the fiction of Hans von Grimmelshausen. However, as in the case of *Joseph Andrews*, no other strategy can bring so completely into play the critical inquiry into the way in which such a chapter does, though perhaps in a perverse way, become a part of the whole. For either chapters enlarge our sense of expectation and fulfillment, either they intelligibly divide an artistic whole, or they have no excuse for being. And even Beckett, as he himself surely knows, creates order as he denies it by making a novel out of chapters.

8
Chapter Against Chapter

IN THE EARLY editions of *The Wild Palms* and *The Old Man*, Faulkner arranged the chapters of each short novel alternately, so that a chapter of one follows a chapter of the other. There is a certain similarity of tone between the two works, and a certain contrast in their philosophical import. *The Wild Palms* works toward a kind of grim nihilism while *The Old Man* achieves an impressive human affirmation. But these relationships, if relationships they are, are all that exist to connect the two works. There is no explicit relation between their action; there is no particular similarity between their dramatic structures; a climax in one does not coincide with a climax in the other. They are two dissimilar and independent novellas, and their typographical juxtaposition would seem to be grounds for accusing Faulkner of that avant-garde flamboyance which, for all his dignity and high seriousness, he sometimes indulged in—a meretricious device, in other words, aimed at giving a facile illusion of something new.

Rereading the two novellas separately, however, in comparison with one's recollection of them in their original alternating form, as they are customarily reprinted, can be slightly disappointing, but not because of any diminished pleasure in the works. The experience can be disappointing because of the loss of the peculiar pleasure which the alternating chapters can provide. J. L. Styan has described a kind of modern drama, analogous in certain ways to the violent alternations of Faulkner's chapters, and his description goes some distance toward accounting for the effectiveness which it is possible to feel in reading Faulkner's alternating chapters. "Dark comedy," Styan wrote,

is drama which impels the spectator forward by stimulus to mind or heart, then distracts him, muddles him, so that time and time again he must review his own activity in watching the play. In these submissive, humiliating spasms, the drama redoubles its energy, the play's image takes on other facets, the mind other aspects, and the spectator "collects the force which again carries him onward." But now progression is more cautious, and he is on guard. He is charged with a tension as a result of which he is a more alert and therefore responsive participant. This tension is one of dramatic irony.[1]

William Empson, too, described the effects of double plots in ways that potentially illuminate Faulkner's chapters. Double plots, he stated, give the appearance that the work deals with life as a whole, they effect a "marriage" of two opposed and complementary myths, and they increase the possibilities for irony.[2] From one point of view, perhaps, the effect of Faulkner's chapters is no different from the effect of reading alternate chapters in different works—a chapter of *Persuasion* followed by a chapter of *Women in Love*. But the fact is that Faulkner's chapters are contained within the same hard covers; they carry with them his implicit intention to arrange them in just that way; thus they compel the reader's attention in a way that an arbitrary juxtaposition of chapters does not.

We are accustomed to thinking of fiction progressing by a kind of dramatic logic from chapter to chapter, each new

[1] *The Dark Comedy: The Development of Modern Comic Tragedy* (Cambridge: Cambridge University Press, 1962), pp. 251–52.

[2] *Some Versions of Pastoral* (Norfolk, Conn.: New Directions, 1960), pp. 25–84.

unit growing inevitably out of the units that have preceded it. The word *continuity* has occurred so often in these discussions because it is the one abstract quality that is likely to seem, in an a priori way, indispensable for good fiction. The conventions of chapter division provide a means by which an effect almost the opposite can be achieved, a narrative in which the chapters do not modulate from one to the other but, rather, deliberately work against each other, producing that tension, energy, and irony which Styan attributed to modern comic tragedy.

The Satyricon of Petronius is surely one of the prototypical examples of the use of discontinuity in fiction. "If the characters are realistic," wrote William Arrowsmith, "they also reach out for the fabulous; if they mock one another, they are in turn mocked by what they are or by their placement in a narrative situation. And the condition of these ironies is the crisscrossing of crucial perspectives and incongruous styles: if we see how the realistic undercuts the fabulous, we should also see how the fabulous sometimes emerges from the realistic." [3]

The tradition of which Petronius forms a part, however, if there can be said to have been one, was pre-novelistic. The contrasts, the shocks, and the discontinuities do not operate ironically and perversely against a realistic tradition of narrative prose. Thus the chapter, as a narrative unit, has little to do with the stylistic and satiric virtuosity of Petronius. His transitions from chapter to chapter are as smoothly modulated as any in the most soberly realistic novel. The abruptness and discontinuity are within, rather than between, the chapters, by way of burlesque of some kind of pastoral melange then fashionable, rather than burlesque of the tech-

[3] *The Satyricon*, Mentor Edition (New York: New American Library, 1960), p. ix.

nical sequence of chaptered narration. It would seem reasonable to assume that the radical disarrangement of chapters, as chapters, is a result of a long tradition of narrative conventionality which the writer feels is not only inadequate to his own imaginative vision but which is in itself an object of the writer's satire. Insofar as one can legitimately speculate about a work so fragmentary and so remote, it is reasonable to assume that the slender tradition of narrative prose before Petronius provided him with no such body of conventions regarding the proper sequence of the units of a narrative, for if he had felt the pressure of such conventionality, he almost surely would have extended his comic discontinuity to the transitions between his chapters and in fact to the substance of the chapters as ordered and sequential units.

By mid-eighteenth century, many of the formal conventions of the novel had been firmly established, among them the way to write epistolary fiction. In Richardson's *Pamela* and even more masterfully in his *Clarissa* a sense of clarity in the order of the action is never absent, despite the multiple narration. The locus of the narrative is always completely clear in time, in space, in point of view. Every letter makes an intelligible link with the letter that precedes it and makes technical and narrative sense in relation to those that follow. In contrast to Richardson's technique, Smollett, in *Humphry Clinker*, began not with a direct exposition of the central conflict of the novel but in this way:

To Dr. LEWIS

DOCTOR,

The pills are good for nothing—I might as well swallow snowballs to cool my veins—I have told you over and over, how hard I am to move; and at this time of day, I ought to know something of my own constitution. Why will you be so positive?

In the course of his letter, Matt Bramble alludes to "my niece Liddy," "Those children of my sister," "Williams," "Barnes," "Griffin," "Prig," and "Morgan." Richardson's conventions lead the reader to expect that the second letter will be either a reply to the first or a letter from one of the persons mentioned in the first letter, amplifying the situation alluded to there. Instead, the second letter is a barely literate communiqué from someone named Tabitha Bramble to Mrs. Gwyllin, housekeeper at Brambleton-hall. Tabitha seems not to have been addressed or alluded to in the first letter. Or is she "my sister"?

The letter, vastly different in tone and diction from the first, mentions preparations for traveling to Bristol, as does the first letter. Does this mean that Matt, the author of the first letter, and Tabitha, the author of the second, will be traveling together? There is a common reference in both letters to an "Alderney cow." But no one who is mentioned in the first letter is alluded to in the second. Instead, the second letter alludes to another person, "that hussy, Mary Jones."

The third letter is addressed to "Mrs. Mary Jones," from "Wm. Jenkins." From the subject matter, it becomes evident that both writer and recipient are servants at Brambleton-hall. But no direct allusion is made to anyone mentioned before. "The squire" is mentioned. Is he the Matt Bramble of the first letter? "Mistress" is mentioned. Is she the Tabitha of the second letter? The third letter, like the first two, refers to a trip to "the Hot Well," but far from providing the key by which all three letters make sense, the third letter is as obscurely related as the second. It is further complicated by being as full as the second letter of solecisms and malapropisms. "Mistriss was taken with the asterisks, but they soon went off," writes Wm. Jenkins. And we may make of it what we will.

Ultimately the fourth letter helps to put all of these people into some intelligible relationship. But not until it has begun and gotten well under way, in a tone far different from any of the first three. "Jer. Melford," of whom we have not yet heard, writes to "Sir Watkin Phillips, Bart. of Jesus college, Oxon.":

As I have nothing more at heart than to convince you I am incapable of forgetting, or neglecting the friendship I made at college, I now begin that correspondence by letters, which you and I agreed, at parting, to cultivate. I begin it sooner than I intended, that you may have it in your power to refute any idle reports which may be circulated to my prejudice at Oxford.

The style here is smooth, cultivated, almost Addisonian. And again the focus and the direction of the narrative are deliberately incongruent, Melford's letter making no visible connection with anything that has gone before.

Humphry Clinker is not a difficult novel, and the reader does get his bearings soon enough. But the narrative conditions are different in kind from Richardson's and from most if not all epistolary fiction which has followed Smollet. In *Humphry Clinker* the narrative break, the separable unit, becomes a means by which Smollet took account of a degree of human variety impossible to him in the continuous picaresque form, despite the abundance of invention in his picaresque novels.

In *Clarissa* there is a central and powerful difference between the moral and rhetorical styles of Clarissa, Lovelace, Jack Belford, and Anna Howe, as there is between the correspondents in the French masterpiece of epistolary fiction, *Les Liaisons Dangereuses*, by Laclos. In Ring Lardner's "Some Like Them Cold," epistolary clichés are exploited for their wildly comic effect, as they are in Smollett, and the story is given its human significance by the growing disparity between the viewpoints of the correspondents. But neither Richardson nor Laclos nor Ring Lardner had a correspondent start off in a direction having nothing whatever to do with the previous correspondence.

To recall Empson's remarks on double plots, Smollett's novel appears to deal with life as a whole, embracing with equal enthusiasm sickness and health, intelligence and stupidity, moral responsibility and moral anarchy, the aristocracy, the bourgeoisie, and the proletariat. Any number of myths are married in *Humphry Clinker*, as Empson suggested is possible with double plots—for example the "poor but honest" myth that surrounds Humphry and the myth of joyous and nearly uninhibited sensuality in Winifred, a modest version of the Fanny Hill myth. It is doubtless significant of the unity in diversity which the novel effects that Humphry and Winifred are actually married at the end of the novel. Thirdly, as Empson wrote, double plots heighten the possibilities for irony. In Smollett's novel, the diversity of narrations underlies the ironic unreliability of each individual narrator, and the comic virtuosity of the novel is a direct result of its ironic contrasts. All of this does not, of course, make *Humphry Clinker* a better or even a more complex novel than *Clarissa*, but different it certainly is. Its own sub-genre is defined by its discontinuity, and without Smollett's exploitation of the possibilities for discontinuity latent in the very division of a narrative, *Humphry Clinker* would be a lesser work.

Kierkegaard's *Either/Or* suggests some rather different purposes for which the narrative units of a fictional work may deliberately act against each other. In Kierkegaard's own terms, much fiction of permanent value is Hegelian. Its resolution is roughly analogous to Hegel's synthesis, a preservation of alternatives in a solution to their contradiction which grows out of the alternatives, includes them, and at the same time reconciles them. *Tom Jones* contrasts constraint with vitality but works toward a conclusion which contains both. *Emma* contrasts pride and intelligence with self-effacement and humility; the synthesis includes both yet reconciles them. *A Portrait of the Artist as a Young Man*, to shift centuries, does not affirm the secular at the expense of the spiritual; it effects a synthesis in which both are embraced. For Kierkegaard, on the other hand, it is choice, not synthesis, which is ethically legitimate, and fiction which realizes this principle will pose legitimate but partial alternatives, rhetorically stressing their attractiveness and certainly implying the necessity of a choice, but without suggesting either a proper answer or the possibility of a reconciliation.

Of *Either/Or*, Kierkegaard, in his stance as ostensible editor, wrote: "One sometimes chances upon novels in which certain characters represent opposing views of life. It usually ends by one of them convincing the other. Instead of these views being allowed to speak for themselves, the reader is enriched by being told the historical result, that one has convinced the other. I regard it as fortunate that these papers contain no such information." [4]

A philosophical mode, then, becomes for Kierkegaard a structural principle. To provide transition between the two halves of *Either/Or* would be to relieve the reader, in part, of his responsibility for making a choice. Not only are the halves of *Either/Or* played off against each other; so, too, are the chapters themselves. "B" 's letters—the "or"—are linked with an almost exaggerated coherence. "Each of these letters

[4] *Either/Or*, Anchor Edition (Garden City, N.Y.: Doubleday, 1959), I, 14.

presupposes the one preceding, and in the second letter there is a quotation from the first; the third letter presupposes the other two." But in the case of "A"—the "Either"—"I have left them in the order in which I found them, without being able to decide whether this order has any chronological value or ideal significance" (pp. 7–8). Thus, the *"Diapsalmata"* comes first, a collection of aphorisms which are fragmentary and often brilliant. "The Immediate Stages of the Erotic" follows, an essay on esthetics taking Mozart as its starting point. After this comes "The Ancient Motif as Reflected in the Modern," an essay significantly subtitled "An Essay in the Fragmentary Read before a Meeting of the SYMPAR-ANEKROMENOI." And so the volume goes, ending with the "Diary of a Seducer." The arrangement, the contrasts, and the pseudo-editorial remarks of Kierkegaard all suggest that he was keenly aware of the power of the narrative convention which dictates that a fiction be divided in a way that is clearly sequential, coherent, and developmental. His practice suggests just as clearly that the way to Kierkegaard's truth lay in the flamboyant violation of the convention.

The narration of much modern fiction is ironic, "unreliable" in Wayne Booth's phrase that bears so heavily upon his argument in *The Rhetoric of Fiction*, and the form of much modern fiction is "open" in Robert M. Adams' phrase alluded to earlier. In these two senses, most modern fiction projects one half of the either/or, that is, an "inside" version of a character's experience which the author will not judge and does not permit to be resolved. Joyce Cary's trilogies extend this principle, becoming "either," "or," and finally a third view of experience, unmediated and unreconciled. But to organize the units of a single fiction according to Kierkegaard's principle of discrete contrast requires a special audacity. It is the audacity one finds, in different ways, in Hesse's

Steppenwolf and Faulkner's *As I Lay Dying*. It is the audacity one finds supremely realized in the brilliant exercise in the construction of a discrete double vision, Nabokov's *Pale Fire*.

Even when structural contrast is not a function of a philosophical method or of an imperturbable ironic poise, as it is not, for example, in the case of Smollett, still its use requires a peculiar sensibility and a special act of will. Disraeli's *Sybil* is about rich and poor, about privilege and distress, about aristocratic polish and proletarian squalor. Its contrasts are intended to be violent. In its own temperate, Tory way, it is an angry book. Yet when, in Chapter iii of Book II, after many pages, Disraeli confronted his proletarians, it is with a modulation so fulsome and so labored as to suggest an imaginative painfulness in the very act of introducing his contrasts.

The situation of the rural town of Marney was one of the most delightful easily to be imagined. In a spreading dale, contiguous to the margin of a clear and lively stream, surrounded by meadows and gardens, and backed by lofty hills, undulating and richly wooded, the traveler on the opposite heights of the dale would often stop to admire the merry prospect that recalled to him the traditional epithet of his country.

Beautiful illusion! For behind that laughing landscape, penury and disease fed upon the vitals of a miserable population.

The contrast between the interior of the town and its external aspect was as striking as it was full of pain. With the exception of the dull high street, which had the usual characteristics of a small agricultural market town, some sombre mansions, a dingy inn, and a petty bourse, Marney mainly consisted of a variety of narrow and crowded lanes formed by cottages built of rubble, or unhewn stones without cement, and, from age or badness of the material, looking as if they could scarcely hold together. The gaping chinks admitted every blast; the leaning chimneys had lost half their original height; the rotten rafters were evidently misplaced; while in many instances the thatch, yawning in some parts to admit the wind and wet, and in all utterly unfit for its original purpose of giving protection from the weather, looked more like the top of a dunghill than a cottage.

"Utterly unfit for its original purpose"—the phrase sounds like the report of a visiting official, which, in a sense, it is. The materialistic detail continues for some pages before any people appear.

This excerpt suggests that, for all Disraeli's anger, an abrupt shift from rich to poor would have been all but imaginatively impossible for him. Part of the difference between Disraeli's approach to his contrasts and our own habits of mind is perhaps the result of the historical development, since the mid-nineteenth century, of sensational journalism and the cinematic montage. But in large part Disraeli's management of the most violent and antipathetic of human contrasts so as to blur and soften their points of contact was a result of his temperament—not an unwillingness to look honestly at the contrasts but an unwillingness to dismiss the possibility of a mediation between them.

Dickens' *Hard Times* is a far more uncompromising novel than Disraeli's and of course a greater one. Dickens saw his contrasts—of beauty and ugliness, power and impotence, wealth and poverty—with a philosophical and human depth that eludes Disraeli. Appropriately, the violence of the contrasts which he saw animates the structure of his novel. The beginnings of Dickens' chapters are overpowering in their directness: " 'Now, what I want is, Facts. Teach these boys and girls nothing but Facts' " (Chapter 1). "Coketown, to which Messrs. Bounderby and Gradgrind now walked, was a triumph of fact; it had no greater taint of fancy in it than Mrs. Gradgrind herself. Let us strike the key-note, Coketown, before pursuing our tune" (Chapter 5). "It was very re-

markable that a young gentleman who had been brought
up under one continuous system of unnatural restraint,
should be a hypocrite; but it was certainly the case with Tom"
(Book II, Chapter 3).

At the end of Chapter 6, Stephen Blackpool leaves Coketown:

So strange to turn from the chimneys to the birds. So strange
to have the road-dust on his feet instead of the coal-grit. So
strange to have lived to his time of life, and yet to be beginning
like a boy this summer morning! With these musings in his mind,
and his bundle under his arm, Stephen took his attentive face
along the high road. And the trees arched over him, whispering
that he left a true and loving heart behind.

At the beginning of the next chapter, James Harthouse is
seen as a quintessential political opportunist, an image introduced without transition or modulation of any kind.

Mr. James Harthouse, "going in" for his adopted party, soon
began to score. With the aid of a little more coaching for the
political sages, a little more genteel listlessness for the general
society, and a tolerable management of the assumed honesty in
dishonesty, most effective and most patronized of the polite
deadly sins, he speedily came to be considered of much promise.

Novelists have always felt themselves free to shift their
scenes from chapter to chapter. And most novelists have always found a certain esthetic usefulness in making these
scenic shifts particularly contrasting. The difference between
Hard Times and the usual structural conventions of traditional fiction is not one of kind but of intensity. Rather than
the small adjustments, the imaginative shifts, and the minor
surprises that chapter divisions conventionally demand of the
reader, Dickens used his beginnings and endings as devices
for intensifying his vision of a divided world. Unlike Disraeli's
structures, we are not introduced to Coketown by degrees,

with tact and patience and understanding. We are placed in its midst, always so as to induce us to feel its violation of Stephen's innocence, Jupe's human warmth, and Louisa's pathos.

It was mentioned previously, in passing, that film techniques, especially the montage, have subtly and probably indirectly modified techniques of fiction. Although newsreel techniques are to some extent prior to analogous fictional techniques and are thus probably causal of the latter, both are part of a shift in sensibility, or are at once result, manifestation, and exploitation of that sensibility, a comment upon and evaluation of it.

Erich Kahler documented such a new sensibility by quoting Ernst Jünger: "'Photography retains with the same impassivity a bullet in its flight and a man who is being torn by an explosion. This now is our peculiar way—a very cruel way —of seeing things; and photography is just an instrument of this peculiarity of ours. . . . We have a queer tendency— difficult to describe—somehow to endow a live happening with the character of a laboratory preparation. Wherever an event occurs in our sphere, it is surrounded by camera objectives and microphones and lighted by the exploding flares of flashbulbs.' " [5] A page later Kahler added a comment from Erich Fromm, in *Escape from Freedom*, on the newsreel: " 'Newsreels let pictures of torpedoed ships be followed by those of a fashion show . . . because of all this we cease to be genuinely related to what we hear . . . our emotions and our critical judgment become hampered, and eventually our attitude to what is going on in the world assumes a quality

[5] Erich Kahler, *The Tower and the Abyss: An Inquiry into the Transformation of the Individual* (New York: Braziller, 1957), pp. 92–93. The quotation is from Jünger's "Uber den Schmerz," *Blätter und Steine*, 2nd ed. (Hamburg, 1942).

of flatness and indifference. In the name of 'freedom' life loses all structure; it is composed of many little pieces, each separate from the other and lacking any sense as a whole.' "

Kahler added his own analysis of *Life* magazine and a forerunner of *Life* in Germany in the 1920's called *Der Querschnitt*, pointing out how their alternations of precisely photographed scenes of misery and personal grief with scenes of fatuous pleasure and consumer goods project the new sensibility. The capacity of modern means of communication and mass media to report worldwide occurrences instantaneously, Kahler continued, constitutes a *"mass production of events."* "The result of all this is a crowding of events in the domain of our vision and consciousness, an oppressive closeness and overwhelming shiftiness of events, an excess of details and complexities in every single event—in short, what I would call an *overpopulation of the surfaces.* And so the sharpest contrasts and phenomenal discordancies, contrasts as sharp as the contrast between nature and machine, have become the normal fare of our daily life" (pp. 95–96).

The value of Kahler's description lies in its joining of the artistic and the sub-artistic, the deliberate and the uncalculated, into a single indictment of modern culture, a chilling view of the phenomenon of discordant structures as unwitting projections of a shapeless, depersonalized life order, participants in and promoters of a kind of maniacal dance of detail. It is no surprise that the highest art and the most debased *kitsch* present structural effects that are rather similar. Indeed, it has been argued that the novel has always drawn its vitality from sub-artistic forms,[6] a thesis that has intriguing possibilities for much fiction from the true crime stories of

[6] Such a view, derived from the Russian formalists, is considered in Chapter 17 of René Wellek and Austen Warren's *Theory of Literature* (New York: Harcourt, Brace, 1949).

Defoe to the use of sensational journalism and fourth-rate popular music by Joyce. In any case, the abrasive fragments of our world of headlines, newsreels, and picture magazines, together with the sensibility which they project and minister to, find artistic reflection in dozens of novelists who seek to understand the structural disorder they present. The most obvious example, and still the most striking example, is Hemingway.

Explicitly developed progressions between narrative units imply a great deal, one hardly realizes how much until one notes their absence: they imply a coherence within the fictive world that is physical, epistemological, and moral. Most of these coherences Hemingway did not believe in and would not counterfeit. The interchapters of *In Our Time*, in their relation to the stories that occur between them, are examples of a lack of faith in coherence made into a structural principle. They remain nearly as shocking now as they were when they were published because they represent no mere overpopulation of surfaces, no mere search for the thrill of contrast, but a controlled and considered artistic structure.

The kid came out and had to kill five bulls because you can't have more than three matadors, and the last bull he was so tired he could hardly get the sword in. He could hardly lift his arm. He tried five times and the crowd was quiet because it looked like him or the bull and then he finally made it. He sat down in the sand and puked and they held a cape over him while the crowd hollered and threw things down into the bull ring.

The above excerpt is about half of "Chapter IX." This is what follows:

MR. AND MRS. ELLIOT

Mr. and Mrs. Elliot tried very hard to have a baby. They tried as often as Mrs. Elliot could stand it. They tried in Boston after they were married and they tried coming over on the boat. They did not try very often on the boat because Mrs. Elliot was quite sick. She was sick and when she was sick she was sick as Southern women are sick. That is women from the Southern part of the United States.

Hemingway's narrative sequence demands the most violent of adjustments of the reader's sensibilities while in effect denying the legitimacy of the motive that seeks coherence, continuity, and transcendent meaning. But one of the ways by which Hemingway avoided the appearance of being overwhelmed and in fact victimized by the incoherence presented is by the use of controlled and precisely poised narrative units. It would not be difficult to compile a list of a score of writers —the work of Donald Barthelme will do for a recent example —who have tried, since Hemingway, with varying success, the same combination of control and incoherence. For it is a strategy which projects the ancient stance of the writer, at once of his time and opposed to his time, and it involves the reader in a strange kind of discomfort in which his sense of order and cause are deeply shaken, but his sense of the power of art to give us an image of our fragmented lives is confirmed.

IV
The Shaping Imagination

9
Anticipation and Realization

—————•—————

IN A LETTER written in 1866 to a now forgotten novelist, Dickens wrote with the authority of experience on the difficulties of serial division:

If you will take any part of [your manuscript] and cut it up (in fancy) into the small portions into which it would have to be divided here for only a month's supply, you will (I think) at once discover the impossibility of publishing it in weekly parts. The scheme of the chapters, the manner of introducing the people, the progress of the interest, the places in which the principal places fall, are all hopelessly against it. It would seem as though the story were never coming, and hardly ever moving. There must be a special design to overcome that specially trying mode of publication, and I cannot better express the difficulty and labour of it than by asking you to turn over any two weekly numbers of A *Tale of Two Cities*, or *Great Expectations*, or Bulwer's story, or Wilkie Collins,' or Reade's, or *At the Bar*, and notice how patiently and expressly the thing has to be planned for presentation in these fragments, and yet for afterwards fusing together as an uninterrupted whole.[1]

What Dickens' letter suggests is that, even if one grants the necessity for chapters as a way of ordering the materials of fiction, there is still an almost infinite number of choices open to the novelist concerning how the continuity of his novel will be divided. The craft of division is especially noticeable, of course, in the serial novelists, with their adjustments

[1] Letter to Mrs. Brookfield, 20 February 1866, *Letters* (London: Chapman and Hall, 1880), II, 249.

to the prior claims of space and periodic interruptions and their consequent management of the interest and pace of the narration. Yet in all novelists, serial or not, the precise point of division which makes the chapter must be a new challenge each time the necessity for choosing it occurs. For dividing the continuity of a narrative is an act which can be done well or badly, as Dickens maintained, and, as he further suggested, to do it well is to enhance the interest and the formal design of the novel while to do it badly is to dissipate its power.

A novel can delay the introduction of its main characters, its main locus, or its main conflicts. Most chapters, on the other hand, establish certain dramatic premises soon after they begin. A chapter gives us our bearings, ordinarily, by introducing a conflict, describing a new place, beginning a conversation, resuming a temporal account after a lapse in time. Once the novelist has given us our bearings, every possibility is open to him. He may exhaust what is implied in his premises; he may resolve his premises yet continue the chapter; he may leave the premises of the chapter deliberately unresolved; he may alter the premises of his chapter; or he may deliberately confuse our sense of what the chapter is about, surreptitiously denying the necessity of fulfilling our expectations at the end of the chapter. None of these possibilities is better a priori, of course; but after the fact, a sense of what else the writer might have done with a chapter, granting his beginning, can confirm our sense of any novelist's craft or of his ineptitude.

Chapter XXIX of Smollett's *Peregrine Pickle* is entitled "He projects a Plan of Revenge, which is executed against the Curate." [2] It begins as follows: "Our hero, exasperated at the villainy of the curate in the treacherous misrepresentation he had made of this reencounter, determined to practice

2 Everyman Edition (London: Dent, 1930), I, 144–48.

upon him a method of revenge, which should be not only effectual, but also unattended with any bad consequence to himself. For this purpose he and Hatchway, to whom he imparted his plan, went to the alehouse one evening, and called for an empty room." And so the plan is carried out: Tunley the landlord is made to suspect the infidelity of his wife with the curate, whereupon he ambushes the curate, beats him, bites his ear, and returns home with his nostrils flaring. Here he gives an account of the beating to Pickle and Hatchway, remains still while his wife contemplates receiving the curate, and leaves the room. "Next day it was reported, that Mr. Sackbut had been waylaid, and almost murdered by robbers, and an advertisement was pasted upon the church door, offering a reward to any person that should discover the assassin; but he reaped no satisfaction from this expedient, and was confined to his chamber a whole fortnight by the bruises he had received."

Smollett's novel, no departure from traditional picaresque structure, interests the reader not by any progressive plotting but by the recurring demonstration of the resourcefulness of its hero and the fatuity of the individuals and institutions with whom he comes in contact. Thus, prior to the beginning of Smollett's chapter we have come to know intimately the cleverness of Pickle and Hatchway; we suspect that no curate, certainly not one named Sackbut, with its comic aura and its suggestion of a primitive trombone, will be a match for him. The premises of the chapter are as clearly stated as possible: the chapter is to be about Pickle's revenge on a curate. In that provisional sense in which the word can be used of literature, Smollett's chapter *exhausts* its premises. It fulfills completely the expectation which it arouses with a symmetry and economy which is rarely possible outside episodic fiction. More is to be heard of the curate in the next chapter. Might that further material have been included in Chapter XXIX? To extend and alter the premise of the chapter would not only undermine that consistency and symmetry which Smollett obviously sought; it would establish the importance of Sackbut. And Sackbut is not important. The fictional unit does not exist for his sake; it exists for the sake of the joke, and with the resolution of the joke, the chapter ends.

It is almost obvious that, though such a chapter as XXIX is typical, it cannot be paradigmatic. Episodic though it be, *Peregrine Pickle* cannot be made out of episodes all of which are as clearly begun, as efficiently described, and as conclusively ended as Chapter XXIX. The novel would become intolerably monotonous, schematic, diagrammatic, mechanical. Hence, even in so uncomplicated a novel as *Peregrine Pickle*, the division of the chapters is various and sometimes, indeed, rather subtle.

Chapter XXVII, for example, begins with this sentence: "As they traveled at an easy rate, they had performed something more than one-half of their journey, when they were benighted near an inn, at which they resolved to lodge." Such an opening sentence arouses classic anticipations: the chapter will contain, one expects, that mid-journey inn scene characteristic of dozens of neo-picaresque novels, with some variety of crankish conversation, some eating and drinking, quite likely some amorous adventure, at least possibly a fight, after which the travelers will leave to complete the last half of their journey. Predictably enough, the chapter continues with some carousing after which the principals go to bed. Unpredictably, however, they are awakened by a fire; Pickle and Pipes, his waggish companion, save Emily, Pickle's beloved, and her friend Sophy, whereupon they are rewarded by gratitude, embraces, kisses, and declarations of love. It is by now morning, so the travelers discharge their bill and resume their journey.

The chapter up to this point has been made out of a combination of the familiar and the surprising. It contains elements reminiscent of Fielding, and the fire may remind the reader of that far different fire scene in *Clarissa*. But for all its familiarity, it is not quite the inn scene we had been led to anticipate. The chapter begins as if its emphasis were to be social, but we see little of the innkeeper and the other guests. Its emphasis turns out to be emotional, narrow, intense, even erotic: "Peregrine put on the ring with great eagerness, mumbled her soft white hand in an ecstasy which would not allow him to confine his embraces to that limb, but urged him to seize her by the waist, and snatch a delicious kiss from her love-pouting lips." The chapter thus extends itself in directions that are implicit and plausible but unexpected. When morning arrives and the bill is paid, the reader expects the chapter to end, both because, in a novel of the road, returning our attention to the road arouses anticipations of a transition to a new episode and because, in the sense of Chapter XXIX, Smollett had made an episode, with its own beginning, albeit a vague and tentative one, its own middle, and its own emphatic end. But the chapter continues.

One reason, it would appear, that the chapter continues is for the sake of the novel's rhythm. The chapters in the Everyman Edition of *Peregrine Pickle* average about six pages in length. In Chapter XXVII, by the time the travelers are ready to set out again, only three pages have elapsed. Thus Smollett was obviously faced with the alternatives of extending his chapter in some way or of leaving it a conspicuously short chapter. The importance of a rough consistency in chapter length varies, surely, from one novelist to another.

However, consistency seems to have been important to Smollett, and, in any case, to have enclosed one of the most intense and dramatic scenes in the whole novel within an extraordinarily short space would have been to detract from its appearance of significance.[3]

In the second half of the chapter, the travelers arrive at their destination, and Pickle is introduced to Godfrey, Emily's brother, who is arrogant and condescending to him. Thus Godfrey comes to stand for the prohibitions and inhibitions that Emily's family display and that separate Pickle from Emily. Ultimately, Pickle extracts warm professions of love from Emily. And "after mutual promises, exhortations, and endearments, Peregrine took his leave, his heart being so full, that he could scarce pronounce the word *Adieu!* and, mounting his horse at the door, set out with Pipes for the garrison." By the end of the chapter, the reader has quite forgotten that the chapter began with anticipations of a standard inn scene. The chapter has become, in effect, two chapters.

Smollett's double chapter evokes two professions of love from Emily in contrasting, almost antithetical, situations. It demonstrates Peregrine's passion, again in two contrasting situations. It combines an act of physical courage with a passage of physical restraint, a situation of dominance with a situation of submission. Thus the chapter establishes at once the fact of Emily's love and the necessity of her separation from Pickle. The chapter begins as a standard inn scene because we cannot be allowed to anticipate Peregrine's courage in the fire and Emily's expressions of love; if these are

[3] Even though no one has considered uniformity in the scale of chapters as a special problem, esthetics is full of discussions that could be made to bear on the problem, discussions having to do with the primal motives that lie beyond rhythm, repetition, balance, and proportion. See, for example, Wilhelm Worringer's *Abstraction and Empathy*, pp. 64–77.

predictable, they lose all force. The chapter cannot be divided with the return of the principals to the road, for to divide it there would be to imply a subordinate completeness to the fire scene and thus to suggest that Emily is more accessible than she really is.

What Smollett forced the reader to do is to adjust his perception of pattern twice, however passively and half-consciously this adjustment may be made: first, to perceive that the organizing principle of the chapter is not, as it seems, comic invention at a rustic inn begun and ended by traveling, and, secondly, to perceive that the organizing principle of the chapter is not the display of a spontaneous, disengaged love between Peregrine and Emily. It is not until the chapter is nearly over that the reader sees that it does indeed make a unit, calculated to contain both love and restraint, the idyllic and the harshly realistic—as is wholly appropriate to the picaresque form, the passionate moment and the necessity to continue.

The third chapter of Jane Austen's *Emma* also has a double dimension, but it is altogether different from Smollett's chapter. In *Emma* the contrast is not developed out of the first half of the chapter. Rather, the two contrasting dimensions are worked out together, in a kind of counterpoint. The chapter begins with an account of the dull, maudlin social circle of Emma's father, Mr. Woodhouse. At almost exactly the midpoint of the chapter, Harriet Smith is introduced—an interesting, pleasant, very pretty young lady who makes a striking contrast, in the mind of Emma, with the tedious gossips of the early chapter. Emma determines to improve Miss Smith, and the chapter returns to small talk and petty people. It ends in this way:

The happiness of Miss Smith was quite equal to her intentions. Miss Woodhouse was so great a personage in Highbury, that the prospect of the introduction had given as much panic as pleasure —but the humble, grateful, little girl went off with highly gratified feelings, delighted with the affability with which Miss Woodhouse had treated her all the evening, and actually shaken hands with her at last!

As with Smollett, we may ask whether the presentation of the usual gossip of Mr. Woodhouse's evening and the encounter with Miss Smith might not have been made in separate chapters. The answer is that of course they might have been, but with considerable loss both to the interest and the ironic import of the narrative.

After the first paragraph of Jane Austen's novel, there is no chapter in which we do not expect, categorically, a response from Emma (although the rather special fifth chapter does violate that expectation). In the third chapter, the catalog of the banalities of Mrs. and Miss Bates and Mrs. Goddard reinforces our expectation that before the chapter is finished Emma will have asserted independence, imagination, wit, or contempt. The simple narrative act of allowing Emma to emerge from a background of mindlessness gives the chapter, for all its small domesticities, a large measure of suspense. After Miss Smith's entrance at mid-chapter, a lesser artist might have permitted her to occupy the fascination of Emma and then ended the chapter, making a significant contrast between those thoroughly unrewarding companions of the early chapter and the intriguing Miss Smith. But Jane Austen allowed the chapter to play back and forth between the two, underscoring each state of mind by means of the other. This, surely, is one manifestation of what Dickens meant by the capacity of the story to seem to be "moving," where dullness is made interesting by our expectation of a response to it and where that response is made interesting by contrast with the dullness. It is not only the thrust and movement of the narrative that is controlled by the precise dimensions of the chapter, however, but the tone as well.

In locating those aspects of Jane Austen's art which serve as vehicles for her irony, it is customary to speak of her diction, her syntax, her mock sententiousness, and her understatement, her dramatic presentation, her management of point of view, and her indirect commentary. Her techniques of grouping and dividing, though scarcely noticed by her critics, brilliantly serve the same ends. Within the same chapter Jane Austen managed to contain an example of the pride, the egotism, and the wish to manipulate others that we are encouraged to disapprove in Emma together with a concrete and sharply delineated rendering of the social circle against which her self assertion is almost a heroic act. Jane Austen's success in making Emma in the same act both repugnant and admirable is a mark of her ironic poise. But it is also a result of her craftsmanship in organizing a unit of her novel so as to compel us to recognize the virtue of stability in the face of audacity, the virtue of audacity in the face of stability, the virtue of intelligence in the face of stupidity, and the blindness of intelligence in the face of the manipulatable—while above all compelling us to take the side of life, of vitality and spontaneity, against the forces of anti-life.

The large Victorian novels seldom achieve, and seldom strive for, the stylized symmetry of Smollett or the ironic economy of Jane Austen in the making of chapters. Chapter IX of *Bleak House* demonstrates a different rationale of division when a novel is not only inventive but inclusive, when it is made not only of situations that impose themselves upon a central character but of a world which is full of both individuals and institutions, complete with both continuities and pseudo-irrelevancies. Dickens' chapter is entitled "Signs and Tokens," a title that tells us nothing except, perhaps, to suggest something of its multiplicity. "I don't know how it is, I seem to be always writing about myself," begins Esther Summerson, Dickens' alternate narrator. "I mean all the time to write about other people, and I try to think about myself as little as possible, and I am sure, when I find myself coming into the story again, I am really vexed and say, 'Dear, dear, you tiresome little creature, I wish you wouldn't!' but it is all of no use." [4]

Whatever premises Dickens planned to establish are delayed by such introductory commentary. Still, making Esther reflect on her relation to her own narrative act clarifies the tentative and exploratory nature of her own chapter-making insight. Half apologizing for the apparent egocentricity of her own narration, she does not know what her chapter will be about. We would be safe in assuming that whatever the action of the chapter, it will be, in some significant sense, about the understanding of Esther.

In the next paragraph, Dickens established the summary quality of the early chapter. "My darling and I read together, and worked, and practised." "The winter days flew by" "I had never seen any young people falling in love before." "They relied more and more upon me, as they took more and more to one another." The participants in this domestic scene are Esther, Richard, and Ada, all three deeply affected by the proceedings at Chancery that make up the shadowy center of the novel, yet all three, for the moment, sheltered from the ugly and the exploitative. There is some talk of Richard's occupation; apparently he will receive no help from Sir Leicester Dedlock and will have to make his own way. There is some business on the management of money, and still more summary of Richard's character.

[4] Riverside Edition (Boston: Houghton Mifflin, 1956), pp. 85–96.

After two and a half pages, the chapter is still without an *event*, but by this time, even before an event, something of the unity of the chapter has become clear. *Bleak House* is not a domestic idyll. A chapter made of gentle pleasures, growing love, and casual self-examination may make a legitimate unit in another novel but not in *Bleak House*. The novel is about the corruption of individuals by corrupt institutions, and in the world of *Bleak House* there are no islands of domestic tranquility. Whatever the exigencies of division, the chapter would not be likely to end short of a contrasting event because the absence, in a narrative unit, of vulgarity, selfishness, or coarseness would undercut the import of the whole novel. No one expects a chapter to be a microcosm of the whole novel in which it appears. Novels, especially large and inclusive ones, can accommodate the chapter as *entr'acte* without threat to the whole structure. But there is surely a sense in which a chapter central to the main action, extensively developed, and prominently placed, must contain, in small, the values and pressures which go to make the world of the novel at large.

In the present case it is a letter from someone named Boythorn which provides both an event and the intrusion of the large world into the sheltered province of the early chapter. Esther voices her concern, along with that of the reader. "Now, who was Boythorn? we all thought. And I dare say we all thought, too—I am sure I did, for one—would Boythorn at all interfere with what was going forward?" Predictably, sweeping into the room with Boythorn come questions of money, property, and court proceedings; unpredictably, he brings with them a rather touching innocence and a quite accessible tenderness. Esther guesses at a frustrated love in Boythorn's youth, which Mr. Jarndyce confirms. But there the matter is dropped. Relating the incident is not relevant to the unity of the chapter; establishing the basis of Boythorn's tenderness is.

This much could make a legitimate and satisfying chapter. With some appropriate rhetorical gestures, Dickens could have ended at that point with a rather powerful balance: the innocent household which we know must be menaced, contrasted with the blustering Boythorn, almost totally caught up in the world of legal maneuvering, yet maintaining his own core of innocence. The narrative up to this point would have had both a thematic unity and a thematic contrast. And it would have satisfied the need for an event by an entrance both decisive and problematic. However a third of the chapter still remains.

Guppy, the law clerk, delivers a message and stays for lunch. After some preliminary embarrassments, he blurts out a proposal to Esther, in legalese, which Esther declines. Guppy leaves, Esther retires to her room, and there she laughs, then cries, then feels oddly touched. It is perhaps a fitting conclusion to the multiplicities of the chapter for Dickens to deny to Esther the esthetic purity of a single emotion at the conclusion and to suggest that Guppy's proposal, and the entire chapter, is at once comic, tragic, and melodramatic.

There is hardly an antithesis which is not contained within the chapter: sincerity and sham, spontaneity and calculation, self-possession and agitation, love and hate. Yet for all its variety, the chapter is still, at almost every point, concerned with the existence of love in an astonishing variety of forms, in a world which is hostile to love. But the question remains, why the exact proportions of the chapter? Why should Guppy's proposal not be reserved for another chapter? The answer must be that his proposal, though it appears at first to be a kind of coda to the chapter, is actually essential to it since it is Esther's means to an act of understanding.

In a manner not unusual in Dickens' fiction, the image of the world that the novel finally presents must be worked toward by both the reader and many of the characters, not in one progressive vision but again and again. To Esther, the foggy, predatory vision of the world which is presented in the first chapter of *Bleak House* is never self-evident. It is not self-evident to her, as it is to us, that the domestic idyll at the beginning of Chapter IX is fragile. She must come to her own understanding of the perversity of love in a world dominated by commerce and chancery by means of the loosely connected loves of Richard for Ada, of Boythorn, and finally of Guppy, in whose stilted love she is directly involved.

The looseness and variety of the chapter, then, are perfectly consistent with Esther's ingenuous imagination. Its multiplicity, moreover, is a function of the multiplicity of Dickens' world. Finally, however, the justification for the chapter's proportions are thematic and psychological, and to stop short of Guppy's proposal would be to lessen both the completeness of Dickens' view of love and to eliminate that final confrontation which makes the intimacy and depth of Esther's emotional range possible.

In one sense, then, the premises of the chapters are suggested at its start. Beginning with innocence, it must end with experience since there is no perpetual innocence in the world of the later Dickens. In another sense, however, the premises of the chapter are scarcely clear until the last word, when the full dimensions of Dickens' treatment of love and the full depth of Esther's insight are revealed.

So far we have seen some of the classic ways in which division reinforces, even makes possible, the fully articulated artistic vision of novels: to mark a self-contained episode, to extend a series of events into a thematic contrast, to control tone by grouping and juxtaposition, to arrange a narrative complex which is at once thematic contrast, thematic unit, and psychological stage. Nothing would be gained by pursuing these forms through the varieties of fiction since their number must be infinite. That is, if one describes it closely enough, every chapter of every novel achieves whatever unity it contains and justifies the fact of its division in its own, slightly different, way. Rather than a catalog of formal unities, the relation between anticipation and realization should be stressed. For every chapter begins with certain prior expectations, arising both from convention and the portion of the novel that has gone before, and every chapter proceeds to form new expectations as it gets under way. It is in the interplay between expectation and consummate fulfillment, between conventionality and audacity, between stock response and the capacity of the novelist to induce an altogether new response that much of the interest and the vitality of the novelist's art reside. Guppy's proposal is a vivid and quite memorable event in itself, but a significant portion of its success is a result of its inclusion in Chapter IX, where it becomes not a whole configuration in itself (in which case it would seem only a whimsical diversion) but the last event in a large, complicated, passionately conceived pattern.

Thus the art of division, by extending, refining, or modifying our initial sense of what is related and what can be grouped together, becomes a technical means by which the novelist compels the reader to see as he sees.

10
The Proportioned Form

Thackeray, writing on Dumas, reports Dumas's describing himself, "when inventing the plan of a work, as lying silent on his back for two whole days on the deck of a yacht in a Mediterranean port. At the end of the two days he arose, and called for dinner. In those two days he had built his plot. . . . The chapters, the characters, the incidents, the combinations were all arranged in the artist's brain ere he set a pen to paper." [1]

Significantly, it is not only the incidents and the combinations that are envisioned in this imaginative act but the chapters as well. Certainly those matters of expectation and fulfillment illustrated in the preceding chapter must have played a part in Dumas's imaginative projection, but the nature of his act, the structuring of the whole novel before a word was written, suggests an analogy with architecture and implies the possibility of another motive, a strategy in which the proportions of a chapter result from certain transcendent esthetic considerations which can be roughed out by such words as *rhythm, balance, magnitude,* and *proportion.*

The first chapter of Joyce's *Portrait of the Artist as a Young Man* begins: "Once upon a time and a very good time it was." [2] Insofar as the beginning of the chapter suggests anything of the unity of the chapter to come, it suggests that the chapter is to be about infancy. Yet after little more

[1] "De Finibus," *Works* (New York: Harper, 1899), XII, 374.
[2] Compass Edition (New York: Viking, 1957), p. 7.

than a page, an ellipsis occurs and the chapter shifts to an account of adolescence. There is a certain continuity of motifs and symbols, certainly a continuity of temperament, as the chapter continues. Stephen is consistently introspective and sensitive, but his qualities of mind, important as they are, hardly give shape and unity to the chapter. The chapter is interlaced with imperatives, but it is not about compulsion, or obligation, or something of the sort.

The chapter pursues a kind of dialectic between isolation and community with Stephen on the fringe of the playground at Clongowes, for example, alienated by its extroverted coarseness, alternating with Stephen at Christmas dinner, surrounded by relatives. But it would be a distortion of the chapter to take its center to be this dialectic. The impulse to assign a subject, a function, or a thematic value to a chapter which the chapter can "treat" or "exhaust" or "resolve" is incompatible with Joyce's novel since the mind of Stephen is different in every paragraph from what it was in the previous one. This is, no doubt, an overstatement. The argument here is against the almost unavoidable tendency to speak of a unit in an internalized fiction as a "stage," a way of thinking that imposes, in Joyce's case, a stasis upon what is clearly intended as flux.

It is all very well to say, as is often said, that the first chapter marks Stephen's preadolescent childhood. But by what logic of the imagination is the infancy of the first page linked with the schoolboy rigors of the latter pages into some total abstraction called "childhood"? While it is true that the first chapter contains four parts—infancy, Clongowes Wood, Christmas dinner, and Clongowes Wood once again—why stop there? Why not five parts, or six?

These questions have no answers because they are the wrong questions. Joyce's first chapter will not be justified on its own terms, at least in the matter of its length and shape, but by reading back from the whole work to the proportions of the chapter. The reason that Joyce's first chapter is in its present form and shape is that that is how much of childhood Joyce thought it necessary to show in proportion to the imaginative structure of the novel as a whole. The chapter is proportionate to the other chapters. It is balanced in the significance of its time span to the significance of the time of the other chapters and of the whole novel. It is long enough to suggest the continuity of childhood, short enough to suggest restraint and selection.

Stephen Hero, beginning with experience, seeks to translate that experience, with a minimum of shaping, into print. The result is not even particularly striking as a transcript. A *Portrait of the Artist as a Young Man*, on the other hand, begins not with experience but with the number five. Tindall suggests that Joyce, in choosing his five-chaptered structure, may have had in mind the classic form of the drama.[3] In any case, Joyce's division precedes the act of writing itself, like the act of a painter in choosing to paint a triptych. In Joyce's five-chaptered novel, the first chapter turns out to be only two or three pages more than a fifth of the whole work.

Such calculated fictional geometry is rare in older fiction. Jane Austen's novels, for example, are extraordinarily shapely but not, presumably, in imitation of an abstract arrangement. Or Dickens' novels, at another extreme, are patterned and controlled but directed toward formal ends that are anything but geometric.

In a novel such as Joyce's, where the progress is intimately developmental, the prior choice of a symmetrical arrangement is a recognition that the experience of a novel, when it is

[3] William York Tindall, A *Reader's Guide to James Joyce* (New York: Noonday Press, 1959), p. 59.

intensely felt, is likely to appear more satisfyingly understood by the novelist if that experience has undergone the pressure of a wish for balance and proportion. Finally, in Joyce's novel, which becomes at its end an affirmation of art, its poised and intricate first chapter participates not so much in the ragged tradition of prose fiction as it does in the tradition of art in general, including architecture, the drama, and classic symphonic forms.

A further example must come from Conrad, for although there have been more audacious experiments than his in the arrangement of the materials of fiction, no one has succeeded in conveying the impression of an art so serious in that matter of technique under discussion here—nor an art, at the same time, so baffling. *Heart of Darkness* partakes of that impulse, identified in Joyce, to arrange the units of fiction symmetrically and to make them of almost exactly equal size. It contains three nearly equal chapters. The reader must acknowledge the possibility that the pressures of serialization had something to do with the shape of the chapters. *Heart of Darkness* appeared first in *Blackwood's*, in three successive installments. Still, Conrad might have divided each installment into subordinate parts; he might have varied the size of the installments; most significantly, he might have rearranged his novella in any way he had wished when it appeared in book form if he had felt that the pressures of serialization had seriously distorted his intent. The fact that the novella stands in its final form as it appeared in *Blackwood's* suggests that the effect of its serialization upon its division was minimal and that it appeared in three installments because Conrad had decided to make it into three parts.

Heart of Darkness has been submitted, often with real illumination, to structural, symbolic, stylistic, and cultural analyses. It seems no distortion of the work to add another way of looking at it by saying that it is concerned, in a significant sense, with pattern formation. The work begins at dusk, expressing the difficulty of distinguishing forms in the half-light. "The sea and the sky," for example, "were welded together without a joint." [4] Marlow, in a moment, interrupts the reverie of the narrator by a speech beginning with "And," suggesting even an indistinguishable quality about that point at which reflection becomes speech. Other seamen, we find, experience a ship, the sea, or a port as being like all the others. They come to easy conclusions about the nature of the whole by a casual experience of the part. Marlow, on the other hand, will not take easy conclusions in the face of mystery. "To him the meaning of an episode was not inside like a kernel but outside, enveloping the tale which brought it out only as a glow brings out a haze, in the likeness of one of these misty halos that sometimes are made visible by the spectral illumination of moonshine."

Even in a casual recollection of the whole work, one is likely to recall images of maps, cartographic colors, and boundaries both natural and political; images of windows, doors, shutters, halls, and ambiguous passages from one physical experience to another; images of black, white, sun, shade, and darkness; images of acts in which the motive is unclear and the consequence blurred; images of shapes which merge into the surroundings; images of recognitions and surprises, odd meetings and dubious farewells. Every work of fiction is about pattern formation in one sense or another since, in the act of arranging his materials, a novelist implicitly presents the perceptual and conceptual rationale for

[4] *Youth: A Narrative, And Two Other Stories: Heart of Darkness and The End of the Tether*, ed. Morton Dauwen Zabel, Anchor Edition (New York: Doubleday, 1959), p. 67.

organizing experience in the way in which he does. *Heart of Darkness*, however, is concerned with the *difficulty* of gestalt perception. Marlow's narration ends with a question, a puzzle, an ellipsis. And the novella ends with the landscape with which it began, the merged sea and sky, leading to an ambiguous horizon. The whole import of the novella suggests, in a hundred ways, the difficulty of separating figure from ground, whether that figure be a jungle hut or a life's work, whether the ground be a wall of jungle or the moral traditions of Western man.

With such a constant preoccupation, cutting the novella into three neatly plotted, satisfyingly enclosed sections would be an act of imaginative mendacity. Marlow certainly does not believe that his own experience falls neatly into thirds. And Conrad, though he could not abandon the habits of mind by which patterns can be found, would not give in to easy delineations. As Marlow says, after a pause, " '. . . No, it is impossible; it is impossible to convey the life-sensation of any given epoch of one's existence—that which makes its truth, its meaning—its subtle and penetrating essence. It is impossible. We live, as we dream—alone.' " Not dramatic units, not "stages" exactly, not thematic units, the three chapters of *Heart of Darkness* are still different from each other and justifiy the fact of their division.

The first chapter is dominated by a bizarre sense of the comic; the import of the chapter is ominous to be sure, with images of fear and hostility, hunger and death, but it is at the same time, and consistently, comic. If the whole novella is a record of Marlow's quest, as it is sometimes described, there is not much sense of quest in the first chapter. Marlow undertakes his journey because, as he puts it, he has seen "a mighty big river" on a map, and that river has fascinated him "as a snake would a bird—a silly little bird." The employees of the trading company office strike Marlow, and the reader, as being grimly absurd. The doctor is preposterous, Marlow's aunt advises him to wear flannels and write often. The activities of the French steamer are exquisitely pointless as it passes trading posts, the names of which seem to place them in "some sordid farce acted in front of a sinister back-cloth." The colonial company is blasting in order to build a railroad, but to no effect; Marlow avoids a hole which has no apparent purpose. A dying native wears "a bit of white worsted round his neck—Why? Where did he get it? Was it a badge—an ornament—a charm—a propitiatory act? Was there any idea at all connected with it?"

This succession of images is sustained throughout the chapter, ending with the two final images of the immobility of the steamer because of the frustrating lack of rivets and the depressing spectacle of the Eldorado Exploring Expedition. The chapter ends with this paragraph.

I had given up worrying myself about the rivets. One's capacity for that kind of folly is more limited than you would suppose. I said Hang!—and let things slide. I had plenty of time for meditation, and now and then I would give some thought to Kurtz. I wasn't very interested in him. No. Still, I was curious to see whether this man, who had come out equipped with moral ideas of some sort, would climb to the top after all and how he would set about his work when there.

Seen as a whole, the chapter begins with the blandest of imagery, the cruising yawl *Nellie* at rest, moves from there to some large, rambling reflections on the nature of civilization, and then proceeds to that remarkably sustained series of absurdities presented in such a way as to compel us to recognize that, ludicrous as they are, the images imply concerns of the very greatest significance. What makes the chapter a unit, as its last paragraph implies, is the introduction of the idea of Kurtz in the mind of Marlow. The chain of absurdities that make up the first chapter can diminish only when a possibility for some transcendent meaning appears, and the idea of Kurtz supplies that possibility.

It is a long chapter, and one can certainly conceive of its being subdivided. Its unbroken amplitude, however, is a useful way of working out what is implied by the magnitude of those early reflections on civilization. Had it been an adventure story, governed in its structure by travel and incident, it could have fallen easily into smaller units. Marlow's farewell to his aunt could have made a natural ending to such a unit. But it is to large patterns of self-discovery that Conrad is faithful.

Similarly one can conceive of the extension of the chapter, but there is a point beyond which the absurdities of the chapter take over the novella, fixing its meaning. Marlow's experience is not, after all, ludicrous. At a finely perceived point the dominant images of his experience begin to appear to him part of a larger purpose. As with Joyce, that point is adjusted to the prior choice of a three-part structure. And as in most traditional fiction, our sense of the significance of that point is defined not only by the direction of the chapter but by deliberate summary at its end.

Intricate as it is, the first chapter is not likely to strike the reader as being audacious or capricious in its precise dimensions. The shape of the second chapter, however, is considerably less conventional. The second chapter is also roughly a third of the novella, sustaining the balance and proportion of the first chapter without suggesting that those perceptual difficulties described above have been abridged for the sake of tailoring the chapter to a preconceived size. Something of the way in which Conrad's second chapter, for all of its regularity of size, seems anything but perceptually contrived can be seen from its ending. " 'I tell you,' " cries the harlequin whom Marlow has encountered on the bank of the river, " 'this man has enlarged my mind.' He opened his arms wide, staring at me with his little blue eyes that were perfectly round. CHAPTER III I looked at him, lost in astonishment. There he was before me, in motley, as though he had absconded from a troupe of mimes, enthusiastic, fabulous." The narration is continuous from chapter to chapter, we can assume, for the moment, because such continuity best expresses the urgency and the lack of form in Marlow's experience.

The second chapter, as one might expect, presents an imagery less calculatedly absurd, more ominous, more intense than does the first, altogether a much altered tone. Insofar as the idea of Kurtz justifies the end of the first chapter, it comes to control the second, less as a possibility of meaning in a ridiculous world than as the object of a mission. Even the symbolic configurations change from first to second chapter. The images of staring eyes, for example, in the concluding passage quoted above, is the last example of a series of images of the visual act far more intense and frequent than any such imagery in the first chapter.

What has changed, in fact, between Chapters I and II is not simply Marlow's mind, not simply his purpose, but his world—no longer a world of ridiculous agents and preposterous outposts but a world of inscrutable power, impenetrable jungle, and awesome suffering. Although it is through Marlow's eyes that we perceive the intensified and quite different world of Chapter II, Marlow cannot be trusted to understand what he perceives. The second chapter ends without Marlow knowing entirely what has ended, and it seems to end almost accidentally because Marlow has reached an area of self-perception so muddy that it is incompatible with the rhythmic repose which is customary at the ends of units in more traditional fiction.

Undoubtedly the most obvious way of ending the second chapter would have been with Marlow's meeting with Kurtz, but the actual encounter does not take place until many more pages. The absence of the physical encounter, at the end of Chapter II—where a lesser artist might have put it, since so much of the second chapter seems to lead up to that event—confirms the impression that structurally the person of Kurtz is less important than the idea of Kurtz. With a gradually increasing portentousness, the idea of Kurtz has played across Chapter II, shifting from the present back to the origins of Kurtz and forward to Marlow's meeting with Kurtz's "intended." What seems to be no ending at all is, in fact, an ending of the most calculatedly anticlimactic sort, the idea of Kurtz propelled from the mind of the most patent fool imaginable. Other fools speak admiringly of Kurtz, but no other fool does it at the end of a chapter. Other events in *Heart of Darkness* are abrupt and half-finished. But no other event bridges a chapter, with a chief actor frozen for a moment, with staring eyes and waving arms, while the reader passes over white space and begins the new chapter.

If not with the discovery of Kurtz, the second chapter might have ended with the death of the helmsman. The event is followed by Marlow's reflections, it marks a genuine and rather touching end, and it could have been, rhythmically and substantively, adapted quite satisfyingly to the traditions of chapter ending. But it would have implied a unit too easily understood, a figure too easily separated from its ground.

The harlequin, by every principle of traditional fiction, belongs in Chapter III, as long as the discovery of Kurtz is to be delayed beyond Chapter II. He is the most deeply influenced figure thus encountered, the most totally mesmerized by the idea of Kurtz. One can only conclude that the harlequin is included in Chapter II for the sake of its ending, for the magnificent sense of absurdity that his interrupted gesticulations make upon the form of the chapter.

In all his reflections forward in time, Marlow never questions the size and the importance of Kurtz. Even in recognizing the enormity of Kurtz's evil, Marlow does not deny to him in Chapter II the stature of a gigantically impressive will. There are two worlds in the novel—the world of absurdity, pettiness, and ineffectuality in Chapter I and the world of massive will in the person and the effect of Kurtz. Marlow cannot make them come together, but the shape of the chapter does—not in summary, not in Marlow's mind at all, but in the act of division, by which the idea of Kurtz, formally and implicitly, is denied its integrity and its dignity.

To use those categories introduced earlier, the second chapter introduces certain premises, certain anticipations, which it proceeds to fulfill in intricate but intelligible ways. At the point of its ending, however, one realizes that in his strikingly audacious division Conrad has left some large anticipations deliberately unfulfilled while, at the same time, indirectly placing the idea of Kurtz in a framework that suddenly unites every element of the work that has gone before.

Signifying a great deal, Kurtz is still a tale told by an idiot. Some pages later, the manager's boy insolently utters the famous sentence, "Mistah Kurtz—he dead." Structurally, and beyond Marlow's understanding, something of the same undercutting effect is accomplished by Conrad's division. That frozen gesticulation reshapes, in retrospect, the whole significance of the second chapter, and it alters, in a way that no interior event could, one's expectations of the working out of the values of the novella in the last chapter. Poised, balanced, and symmetrical, yet agonizingly honest in the shape of their moral perceptions, Conrad's chapters are models of the art of division.

V
History

11
Historical Conclusion: Pre-novelistic

AT THE BEGINNING of this book, gestalt formation was posed as one way of accounting for the need to make chapters. Although such a link between art and experience can demonstrate that chapters are not facile conventions but take their origins in inescapable psychological processes, the descriptive formulas of gestalt are all but useless when one's point of view becomes historical. One cannot locate the time when man learned to make patterns. The configural imagination is simply a necessary quality of man's humanity. The Kwakiutls described by Ruth Benedict and the preliterates of *The Inheritors*, by William Golding, seek to abstract meaningful configurations from the flux of experience just as surely as does a modern historian or the narrator of James's *Sacred Fount*.

There is a condition, however, which can be located anthropologically and perhaps inferred historically, in which the pattern-making impulse does not act upon experience in ways that are analogous to the organization of narrative. It is what Dorothy Lee has called the "nonlineal codification of reality." [1] To make a chapter is to break a line, the line being spatial, temporal, causal, associative, developmental, and so on. When traversing a narrative line from A to C, stopping at B can be an esthetically significant act. In a culture that

[1] "Lineal and Nonlineal Codifications of Reality," in *Explorations in Communication*, ed. Edmund Carpenter and Marshall McLuhan (Boston: Beacon, 1960), pp. 136–54.

sees no line from A to C, B is simply another point, the significance of which lies in itself, not in its place in the entire line. With such a cultural orientation, chapters are impossible.

Professor Lee's distinction is worth summarizing. Building upon the work of Bronislaw Malinowski, she extended her own studies of the culture of the Trobriand Islanders into their language and the kinds of explanations which they offer for their behavior. There is, she found, no verb *to be* since existence is contained within objects. Similarly there are no adjectives; when the quality of a thing is modified, the thing becomes another thing; quality is contained. "Events and objects are self-contained points; . . . there is no temporal connection between objects." The language of the Trobriand Islanders provides no mechanism for distinguishing past from present, cause from result, stimulus from response, expectation from fulfillment, means from end. Their language provides for pattern formation of a fairly complex and ingenious sort; but such patterns have nothing to do with purposive activity. The Trobriand Islanders do, of course, engage in purposive activity, but they do not think of such activity in lineal terms.

In contrast, nearly every linguistic and perceptual act within our culture presupposes an imagined line: the gestures and transitions of a speaker, the perception of development and climax and significance. Even our tests for sanity, as Professor Lee pointed out, assume that failure to perceive such a line amounts to a radical mental disorientation. But such an automatic lineal organization the Trobriand Islanders do not possess, and with such a nonlineal organization history is impossible, as is causal analysis, climax, and plot.[2]

[2] Robert Graves qualifies Lee's contention in "Comments on 'Lineal and Nonlineal Codifications of Reality,'" *Explorations in*

Whether it is logically defensible or not to transfer the present cultural habits of the Trobriand Islanders to the remote history of Western culture, such a transfer provides a working conjecture. If one looks for the conjectural point at which it became possible and indeed necessary to make coherent, continuous, climactic narratives with their own internal segments, then that point must have been coincidental with the development of the lineal habit of mind that we have come to take so much for granted. Such a point remains conjectural, of course. We have no surviving body of Western writing from the other side of that imagined watershed.

The configural impulse and lineal orientation—the first human, the second cultural—are the two necessary qualities from which the history of narrative chapters originates. From remote antiquity to the beginnings of the novel in the eighteenth century, the mutations of narrative division are as various as the purposes of narrative itself, and one of the reasons that the novel is so rich a genre is that its antecedent forms are so various. But many formal mutations have lived and died with the history of the pre-novelistic genre itself and thus become irrelevant to the discovery of the implicit premises of the rise of the novel. That is, there is little point in searching for the antecedents of novelistic form in folktales such as *märchen* or coarse, cynical verse tales such as *fabliaux* or jest biography or beast allegory, even though all of these are part of a continuous tradition of prose fiction and may, in quite indirect ways, have contributed to the ultimate richness of the novel itself.

Communication, pp. 155–61. He cites, for example, a narrative of the Trobriand Islanders that seems to him coherent and climactic. Still, Graves's argument is with individual points in Lee's presentation and does not undermine her basic distinction.

There are three major traditions of pre-novelist segmentation, however, which influenced the great originators of the
eighteenth century and which continue, directly or indirectly,
to shape narrative organization to the present time. They are
the Homeric example, the biblical example, and the conventions of rhetoric.

The "book" in Homer appears to be the result of several
different conditions under which the text which we now
call Homer's came to exist. Here too, of course, one con-
jectures, but in questions of epic, borrowing authority from
Albert Lord is responsible conjecture. In its oral state,
Homer's earlier renderings of his epic materials, like all oral
poetry, were addressed to a particular audience and thus were
bound by the limitations of such an audience's attention. It
is customary to assert that Homer composed his epics for
performance at a festival. The difficulty, however, in trying
to reconstruct the condition in which Homer's poems existed
in their oral state, as Lord pointed out, is that they are extremely long. And thus one is forced to imagine a festival
performance lasting many days, twenty-four, in fact, if one
accepts the traditional division of Homer's epics as represent-
ing a day's recitation.

Robert Fitzgerald, in the notes to his translation of *The
Odyssey*, has worked his way to conclusions that do not
demand a prolonged duration of days. "A probable rate of
Homeric performance was about five hundred lines an hour.
So far as I know, nobody has gone very far with deductions
from this fact. The first four books of *The Odyssey* are
obviously a narrative and dramatic unit, so are the next four,
and so are the next four. These are three successive waves
of action, and each runs to about two thousand lines or about
four hours of performance. There is no reason for not regard-

ing this as the duration of a formal recital." [3] What Lord suggested, however, is that the poem which we now have is not the poem which was performed. Homer did sing the stories of Achilles and Odysseus at festivals, in considerably briefer versions than those which we now have; however, the text which we now ascribe to Homer was no transcription of such a performance but rather the result of dictation to a scribe. [4]

Thus the *Iliad* and the *Odyssey* are not transitional poems, lying midway between oral and written culture; they are oral in every respect, the product of a singer accustomed to direct performance, aware of his immediate audience, obliged to adapt his form to their capacity to listen. But in their transcription, freed in that one instance from time limits and festive crowds, the poems were allowed to grow and elaborate, to become richer and more various. At the stage of its transcription, then, the structure of any given book in Homer's poem tends to be as long as it is, and its subject matter is so adapted to that length, because that is the duration of attention which the oral poet could expect of his audience. But the pressures of oral recitation, accepting Lord's conjecture, were carried over into a kind of ideal performance, to a silent, attentive, durable, and quite possibly devout scribe, who was willing to listen to as many "days" as the poet wished.

About two centuries before Christ, in the midst of a flourishing cult of Homer, an Alexandrian scholar, probably Zenodotus, first divided the Homeric poems into twenty-four

---

[3] *The Odyssey*, trans. Robert Fitzgerald, Anchor Edition (New York: Doubleday, 1963), p. 494.

[4] Albert B. Lord, *The Singer of Tales* (Cambridge, Mass.: Harvard University Press, 1960), pp. 152–53.

books each.[5] That physical division has remained customary ever since. Whether Zenodotus' division was made on the basis of some previous tradition or not is unknown, but a glance at the present text indicates that such a division was no arbitrary act. In the Fitzgerald translation, the first book of the *Odyssey* ends with one of the most skilful, elaborate cadences in all of narrative literature.

> No servant loved Telémakhos as she did,
> she who had nursed him in his infancy.
> So now she held the light, as he swung open
> the door of his neat freshly painted chamber.
> There he sat down, pulling his tunic off,
> and tossed it into the wise old woman's hands.
> She folded it and smoothed it, and then hung it
> beside the inlaid bed upon a bar;
> then, drawing the door shut by its silver handle
> she slid the catch in place and went away.
> And all night long, wrapped in the finest fleece,
> he took in thought the course Athena gave him.

Clearly, it took no scholarly audacity on the part of Zenodotus to perceive at such a point the intention to seem to end a section of the poem.

A Homeric book, it seems, results from the operation of three forces: the lifelong adjustment of the poet's narrative art to the demands of a direct listening audience; the scribal dictation, if one accepts Lord's supposition, which permitted the adaptation of those oral habits to a new leisured set of dimensions; and the fixity of those natural divisions by the authenticating act of Zenodotus. It is impossible to overestimate the significance of the fact that two of the oldest, greatest, most honored, and most deeply loved of narrative

[5] See Moses Hadas, *Ancilla to Classical Reading* (New York: Columbia University Press, 1954), p. 143.

works come to the post-classical reader with twenty-four sections more or less equal in size, in which the internal form of each section, however traditional, impromptu, and indeterminate it may be, is skilfully adjusted to the size of the section. One can think of no greater authority for the assumption that the way to write an extended narrative is to write it in chapters. Conversely, the heavy sanction of the Homeric book establishes that, in general, to write an extended narrative which is not divided is to appear either primitive and crude or contrary and perverse.

The intrinsic divisibility of the books of the Bible differs, one from another. In Chapter 3, we saw that the first chapter of the Book of Job is a natural division whose end is preceded by a long and powerful cadence. Similar examples can be found at widely separated points. The second chapter of the Gospel according to St. Luke makes a narrative unit, consistent, coherent, and rhetorically enclosed.

Chapter 25 of Genesis is a much less dramatically divided unit. The chapter ends with a certain finality. "Then Jacob gave Esau bread and pottage of lentiles; and he did eat and drink, and rose up, and went his way: thus Esau despised his birthright." Much of Chapter 25, however, has been taken up with genealogy, only about the last third of it involving the selling of Esau's birthright to Jacob. Not even the domestic life of Isaac and Rebecca occupies an entire chapter, since much of the early portion of Chapter 25 is only tangential to it. In no sense is the chapter a rhetorical or substantive unit. Yet its physical division after the sentence above provides a certain emphasis, a sense of completion, and no violation of the flow of the subject matter. The next chapter moves on to matters of famine and the subsequent prospering of Isaac. What one feels, on passing from the twenty-fifth chapter to the twenty-sixth is that the narrative displays no internal impulse to make chapters at all but that the imposition upon the narrative of chapters tends to give it a sense of order and symmetry which it otherwise would not have had.

Chapter divisions of the Bible originated in the Vulgate and are variously attributed to Lanfranc, an Archbishop of Canterbury who died in 1089, to Stephen Langton, who died in 1228, and to Hugo de Santo Caro, who flourished in the thirteenth century.[6] As in the case of Homeric narration, the tradition prior to the actual assignment of chapters must have been various and is impossible to recover. Certainly in the case of some biblical texts there were graphic indications of division. The point, however, is that by the time of the Renaissance, writers of every degree of learning and sophistication had, as part of their common cultural experience, a body of writing including the prophetic, the historical, the poetic, and the homiletic, widely varying in tone and technique, in age and authority, and all of it divided into chapters. To find parallels, analogues, and derivations between biblical division and fictional construction is methodologically difficult and, after all, unnecessary. The shape of the Bible is simply a generalized part of the background of the modern European mind, to be drawn upon in the most indirect and unconscious of ways. And part of the nature of this shape is the chapter, imposed upon every kind of rhetorical material and imposed equally upon those passages whose internal organization implies the necessity for division and those passages whose internal organization implies no such necessity.

David Lodge has remarked that "The writer's medium differs from the media of most other arts—pigment, stone,

<hr>

[6] Ira Maurice Price, *The Ancestry of Our English Bible*, 3rd edition (New York: Harpers, 1956), pp. 36, 185.

musical notes, etc.—in that it is never virgin: words come to the writer already violated by other men, impressed with meanings derived from the world of common experience." [7] It is not only words that come to the writer violated but larger relationships within his medium as well: syntax, rhetoric, and form. Whether language used for exposition differs in an essential way from language used for fiction is still a debatable and debated point. But even if it were true that the language of fiction is radically different from language used for referential purposes, the fact remains that in a general sense, the two mediums are the same and that when a writer uses a word, a sentence, or a rhetorical unit, he must use it knowing that it has a prior validity and a prior usefulness in general referential discourse.

Part of the background of a writer's medium has less to do with usage than with pedagogy. It is not only the way that language is used that limits the way in which a writer may use it, but it is also what we are taught about the way in which it should be used. A writer who has been taught that "The reason is because" is an egregious tautology may observe that the construction appears in the best of writers; but linguistic inhibitions are not always overcome by logic, and such a writer may find the phrase difficult to use long after the schoolroom prohibition has faded from his mind.

The prior background of larger rhetorical forms is not likely to be felt so specifically as it is with individual words and small constructions. It is still true, however, that any writer begins to write a paragraph, in any kind of prose for any purpose, carrying with him certain stylized and pedagogic ideas about

[7] *Language of Fiction* (New York: Columbia University Press, 1966), p. 47. For an excellent summary of many of the debates regarding artistic and referential language, see the early pages of Lodge's volume.

how a paragraph ought to be made. The writer may, of course, make his paragraph in any way that he pleases. But what he cannot do is eradicate his prior absorption of rhetorical prin- ciples. So it is with chapters. When Cicero or Quintilian or any of fifty medieval rhetoricians write of the making of a dis- course into units, their principles have nothing to do with the novel, which did not exist and which most of them would have disapproved of if it had. Yet they impress upon language certain principles and predispositions which remain even when language is used for purposes quite different from what they had in mind.

Quintilian will do for an example, as neither the most exhaustingly ample of rhetoricians nor the tersest, but prob- ably the most influential of them all. An oration, he stated, begins with an *exordium,* though certain other rhetoricians have further divided it into introduction and insinuation. There is no doubt throughout Quintilian's discussion that the *exordium* is not simply a loose and generalized way of talking about the beginning of a discourse but that it is regarded as a psychological unit, intended to impress listeners in a particular way which is distinguishable from the response of listeners to the later sections of the oration. The *exordium* is followed by the *narratio,* or the statement of facts, which is followed by the proof (subdivided into *distributio, confirma- tio, reprehensio,* possibly a *digressio*), which is finally fol- lowed by the peroration. As with *exordium,* these further divisions are not analytic categories, arbitrarily applied to continuous discourse; they are real divisions, different from each other in tone, construction, purpose, and anticipated response. A major part of Quintilian's *Institutes* is given to matters of arrangement and division, to consistency and the possibility of digression, and the number of incidental arguments with other rhetoricians about the terminology of division is staggering.

The primary and secondary bibliography of rhetorical studies from Aristotle to the present is enormous. It requires, in fact, an act of imagination by the modern reader—who is accustomed, let us say, to a slender volume of witty advice on matters of style by Strunk and White—to comprehend the dimensions of classic rhetoric, with its clotted taxonomy, its pompous truisms, and its many, many volumes. It suffices here to suggest that nearly any writer with a smattering of education from Aristotle to the twentieth century would have been predisposed to think of discourse in terms of rhetorical categories and further predisposed to think of a whole discourse in terms of its separable parts.

The example of Chaucer, as a dozen detailed studies show, presents a writer of narrative, intimately conversant with the principles of rhetoric, able to modulate between classic forms of the sermon, classic forms of narrative, and strikingly verisimilar interludes—all of this in such a way as to make the line between exposition and narration quite indistinct and to preserve, in passages of quite divergent character, the influence of the rhetorician.

In an earlier chapter we noted the remarkable progress in the eighteenth-century English novel, seemingly from discovery and exploitation in chapter construction to its parodic demolition in Sterne. To some extent, Sterne's parodic play with the units of fiction was directed against the conventions of his immediate predecessors. But *Pamela* was published in 1740, *Joseph Andrews* in 1742, and the first two volumes of *Tristram Shandy* in 1760. Insofar as Sterne reacted against the eighteenth-century novel, it was at best a twenty-year-old tradition which provided the butt of his jokes, certainly a brief period to justify the full range of Sterne's hilarity.

In a much larger sense, what Sterne parodied was rhetoric, not Fielding and Smollett, two thousand years of solemn theory, not twenty years of prose fiction. No one has yet catalogued all of the rhetorical forms to be found in *Tristram Shandy*, but it is clear that to do so would take a monumental familiarity with classic rhetorical writing. The presence of so many *exordia* and perorations, *aposiepesis* and *paronomasia* (I quote categories at random from Quintilian with considerable confidence that whatever rhetorical category appears there can also be found in Sterne) testifies to the common recognition of rhetorical principles through the eighteenth century and to the power of rhetoric to influence the narrative imagination without which the Sterne's parody would have been quite pointless.

Fielding's fiction further suggests the powerful presence of the three influences sketched here. It is true that the most immediate structural influence upon Fielding was Cervantes, who adopted the episodic divisions of romance but exploited the possibilities of contrast and thematic grouping latent in the fact of division. More than merely ways of propelling interest, chapters in Cervantes' fiction are ways of demonstrating possibility and limitation, motive and action, sense and sensibility, mind and matter. So, too, did Fielding use them. Yet the three classic influences are deeply and fundamentally present as well. The mock epic tone and the remarks on epic books in *Joseph Andrews*, the calculated epic structure in *Tom Jones*, and the elaborate parallels with the *Aeneid* in *Amelia* show a narrative imagination in pursuit of structural effects which derive from the structure of epic. The orthodox Christianity and the fondness for biblical parallels (as in the fashioning of the episode of Joseph and the coach after the parable of the good Samaritan) show an imagination in the process of converting biblical materials to contemporary purposes. Both the depth of Fielding's learning and the breadth of his rhetorical effects reveal an intimate familiarity with rhetorical categories.

The Homeric book, the biblical chapter, and the rhetorical category, then, are the primary means by which the convention of the chapter became, by the eighteenth century, so thoroughly sanctioned, so necessary, so automatic that almost no one thinks to question it.

12
Historical Conclusion: Novelistic

IN EARLIER discussion, we saw two directions in which the technique of the chapter moves through the history of the novel. One is the tendency of progressive, developmental units to replace static or exemplary units. The other is the use of chapter techniques in the hands of certain novelists from mid-nineteenth century to the present to achieve a formal abrasiveness that stands for a lack of cohesiveness which such novelists see in modern culture. In attempting to move beyond these two tendencies toward finer discriminations, one realizes quickly the limitations of the conventional concepts of period style. Such concepts can help to differentiate the mind of Jane Austen from the mind of Meredith, the fictive world of George Eliot from that of Bennett, and the psychological presuppositions of Hardy from those of Virginia Woolf.

In rather elemental matters of form, however, concepts of period style contradict more than they clarify. That open, unresolved, fragmentary forms are typically romantic, for example, is an idea that can readily be supported by scores of nineteenth-century lyric poems. But when one tries to shift that useful generalization about period style from lyric poetry to the forms of the novel, one looks in vain in the romantic period for an exploitation in fiction of openness so thorough as Sterne's. Or if one approaches the question of changing forms from the direction of esthetics, it is obvious and widely verifiable that writers of poetry in the eighteenth century often

173

let form precede subject matter—"imitating" Horace, composing an eclogue, making a typographical poem in the manner of Denham—while poets in the nineteenth century often reversed the order, letting the form be dictated by the pressures of the substance of the poem.

One transfers this generalization to prose fiction to find that it illuminates almost nothing. The novels of Kingsley and Reade in the nineteenth century can be as preordained and as formulaic as any fiction of quality in the eighteenth century. And in any case, such esthetic premises, if they apply to fiction at all, lead to no fruitful observations on the making of chapters. The inconvenient fact is that, until the twentieth century, concepts of period style account for very little in the making of chapters. Beyond those broad directions already sketched, the mutations of the chapter from the mid-eighteenth century to the twentieth can best be approached first by the disturbingly peripheral route of typography and the conventions of publishing, second by some directions in cultural history.

An inescapable wish for proportion tends to compel writers of books to adjust the size of chapters to the dimensions of the bound and finished books themselves. This sounds paradoxical perhaps, since the writing is prior to the publishing and the two are usually altogether separate acts. Yet in any given period, books of a certain kind tend to look more or less physically alike, and thus, in a general way, a writer can imagine the shape of his published book even as the idea of the book is beginning to form itself.

Most histories in the eighteenth century were printed in folio and were divided either into long, rather arbitrary chapters or were not divided at all, their topical progress being indicated by brief marginal designations. Obviously they were intended to be read either here and there, encyclopedia fashion, for information, or to be read in long, unbroken stretches. In contrast, most fiction was printed in smaller format, often in duodecimo, in a size which could be carried, read casually, slipped into the pocket—even, as in *The Rivals*, concealed. *Joseph Andrews*, for example, not a long novel, was published in two duodecimos. *Tom Jones* first appeared in six volumes, *Clarissa* in seven, and *Tristram Shandy* trickled from the press in nine volumes over a period of eight years. Even Sterne's *Sentimental Journey*, which now seems hardly to justify a paperback to itself, appeared in two duodecimo volumes. And both *Pride and Prejudice* and *Sense and Sensibility*, which now fit together into a single Modern Library text, appeared originally in three duodecimo volumes each. To publish in this way is to superimpose a scale upon the subject matter, not rigidly and inflexibly, of course— there are surely some small books with large chapters—but in general.

The point here is that it is less the total length of a novel that tends to determine the size of its units, less its scope or inclusiveness, than the published form which convention leads the novelist to expect his book will take. Further, a two-page chapter in folio would seem disturbingly truncated, but the same chapter spread out to five or six pages duodecimo would seem far more justly proportioned. Designed to be carried and read casually, eighteenth-century fiction was just that. Its audience was wide and diverse, but it included a majority of readers who were not at all leisured, whose attention to a novel must have been shallow.

At any given point, a novelist's decision to divide is a result of artistic pressures within his work, but the general rhythm and frequency of division of the novels in a given period is to some extent the result of both the kind of publishing and the kind of reading the novelist expects. Each of these extra-artistic pressures tended to establish the norm in the eighteenth century and the precedent for the genre ever since, of comparatively brief units, intelligible as units, in which the reader's interest is calculatedly propelled, especially at the point of division.

The single most significant aspect of the publication of fiction in the nineteenth century is serialization. It is an elusive phenomenon, but one can say that it was a major source of anxiety for novelists from Dickens through James. Dickens' advice to another novelist, as it reflected his own experience concerning serialization, was quoted earlier. Similar expressions occur throughout Dickens' private writings, though often with less self-assurance and much more frustration. At the other end of the period, Henry James, in plotting out *The Portrait of a Lady* in his notebooks, remarked to himself: "After Isabel's marriage there are *five* more instalments, and the success of the whole story greatly depends upon this portion being well conducted or not." [1] In scores of cases the proportion, the pace, and the arrangement of fiction in the nineteenth century were affected by such matters as regular deadlines, limited space, and widely interrupted reading periods.

One tends to think of such pressure as being destructive of art, and in certain ways it must have been. Yet it may also have resulted, now and then, in a fiction more controlled and concentrated. As John Butt and Kathleen Tillotson have noted, "Through serial publication an author could recover something of the intimate relationship between story-teller and audience which existed in the ages of the saga and of Chaucer; and for an author like Dickens, who was peculiarly susceptible to the influence of his readers, this intimate rela-

[1] *The Notebooks of Henry James*, p. 15.

tionship outweighed the inherent disadvantages of the system."[2]

As for the relation between the serialization and the conventions of the chapter, it is important to recognize that monthly parts rarely coincided with the single chapter. Of the novels of Dickens which appeared in monthly serialization, most installments contain two chapters, some as many as six, and only rarely does an installment contain a single chapter.[3] What happens, in such cases, is that the rhythm of division is governed by two sets of criteria simultaneously, and though the length of the installment is artificially imposed upon the novelist, the possibility of making chapters within the installment is preserved. What this indicates is that the craft of chapter making was rather less affected by the fact of serialization than one might expect and that much of the traditional rhythm and craft of chapter division could be preserved, however demanding the pressures of the installment may have been. Archibald Coolidge took note of the frequency of the "curtain" at the ends of installments, the ending which builds to a climax yet contains an unanswered question. But he hastened to add that, though this effect is exploited by the serial novelist in general and by Dickens in particular, it is hardly an organizational feature of serial novels alone and appears in all kinds of novels of all periods.[4]

One way of determining the effect of serialization upon the nature of chapters is to take up a volume of Dickens or Thackeray, reading with special attention to its structural

[2] *Dickens at Work* (London: Methuen, 1957), p. 16.

[3] A chart listing the serialization of Dickens' novels appears in K. J. Fielding, "The Monthly Serialization of Dickens's Novels," *The Dickensian*, LIV (January, 1958), 4–11.

[4] *Charles Dickens as Serial Novelist* (Ames, Iowa: Iowa State University Press, 1967), p. 56.

features, its manipulation of suspense, its control of interest, guessing, if one can, where the original monthly parts occur in the bound text in which they are now typographically indistinguishable. If the effect of serialization were conspicuous, then the parts would stand out with all the crudity of effect which has often been alleged. It would seem, however, that distinguishing the parts in this way is extremely difficult. And it would also seem that, though serialization undoubtedly affected the motives and the anxieties of novelists, though it undoubtedly affected the subject matter of novels and the relationship between writer and reader, it affected the construction of the units of fiction in rather minimal ways.

One of Thomas Hardy's novels provides a somewhat different perspective on the problems of serialization. Mary Ellen Chase has documented the differences between serial and finished novel in Hardy, the serial installments being heightened in the interests of sensationalism, modified in the interests of prudery, and rigged in the interests of a superficial sense of drama. For example, she quoted parallel passages from *The Mayor of Casterbridge*, this from the finished novel:

With this view she made a toilette which differed from all she had ever attempted before. To heighten her natural attractions had hitherto been the unvarying endeavor of her adult life, and one in which she was no novice. But now she neglected this, and even proceeded to impair the natural presentation. She had not slept all the previous night, and this had produced upon her naturally pretty though slightly worn features the aspect of a countenance ageing prematurely from extreme sorrow. She selected —as much from want of spirit as design—her poorest, plainest, and longest discarded attire.

The parallel point in the serial reads this way:

With this view she spent the whole afternoon in making a toilette which differed from all she had ever attempted before. To heighten her natural attractions had hitherto been the unvarying endeavor of her adult life, and one in which she was no novice. But now she systematically proceeded to impair the natural presentation. In two hours she had produced upon her naturally pretty though slightly worn features the aspect of a countenance withering, ageing, sickly—a head of hair with a few incipient grey threads; in brief, prematurely wrecked by extreme sorrow.

The chemist up the street, who eked out a meager drug trade by scented soaps, cosmetics, and disfiguring ointments of various kinds, was three or four times requisitioned for this proceeding. By the time she had sicklied herself to her mind the hour had arrived.

It was with a shudder, almost with a terror, that she beheld in the glass what she had done. It seemed too real. If her dear husband should meet her he would surely believe that this was her true aspect, and that her hitherto charming lineaments had been the counterfeit of art.[5]

Every aspect of the making of chapters is bound to be affected when parallel versions differ so radically as these, from the detached austerity of the later version to the breathless effusiveness of the serial. Still, as one is about to generalize on the near-disastrous effects of serialization upon the nineteenth-century novel, one reflects on how little difference it makes after all; one reflects, that is, on the fact that so many of those lapses in taste and art in Hardy's serials were rewritten to tremendous advantage and the fact that it is the novels in book form that one reads. Taking Hardy as a paradigm case, one can assume that the texture, the construc-

[5] Mary Ellen Chase, *Thomas Hardy from Serial to Novel* (Minneapolis: University of Minnesota Press, 1927). The parallel passages are quoted on pp. 37–38.

tion, and the division of certain nineteenth-century novels
were affected by the pressure of serialization; yet considering
Hardy's revised and finished books, the individual installments are no more crude and obvious there than they are in
Dickens' finished novels, and one must assume that the serial
novelists, at least the best of them, found means to preserve
the artistic integrity of their fiction against the pressures of
serialization when those pressures became destructive of their
art.

Middlemarch served earlier to stand for the progressive,
developmental use of chapters and the use of such chapters
not merely because that is the way that George Eliot's mind
worked but because certain movements in cultural history
made it possible for her imagination to work in so developmental a way. *Middlemarch* serves conveniently to suggest
another direction of cultural history which is important in
making chapters. Probably the most frequent critical observa-
tion on that novel concerns its breadth, the multiplicity of
its interests, and the complexity of its account of cause. To
contrast with Fielding, in mid-eighteenth century there were
three options available for showing cause: providence, chance,
and human will. All three can be found in abundance in most
of the historians of the period. But providence, despite Fielding's Christian orthodoxy, does not operate in his fiction.
Chance now and then initiates a long series of events, but it
can hardly be said to operate systematically throughout his
fiction, and it certainly cannot be said to qualify human
responsibility in the least. What happens in Fielding's fiction
happens largely because human beings make it happen, wil-
fully or spontaneously. And the responsibility of the novelist
is to show how this is so.

What happens in George Eliot's fiction is the result of will
and chance. It is also the result of law, religion, social class,

history, geography, education, and a thousand cultural habits of mind, ranging from resistance to change to marital conventions to table manners. What happens in Parliament matters to what happens in Middlemarch. What happens in a Paris medical school matters to what happens in Middlemarch. What happened to Bulstrode twenty years before matters to what happens to him now. And so on, indefinitely.

The most obvious result of this multiplicity of cause is the grouping of chapters in *Middlemarch*. A section of the novel can be entitled "The Dead Hand" because, in a generalized but diverse and pervasive way, the dead hand of the past affects the whole fabric of Middlemarch society, because the legacies of Casaubon and Featherstone affect a large group of people; because all of these people in certain ways affect each other; because further events without direct bearing on the legacies or the legatees will be, in the most indirect of ways, affected by them; because, in a way that we can only begin to foresee at that point, the dead hand of Bulstrode's past has begun to affect him; because, in short, of the interrelatedness and multiplicity of cause in the novel.

Also, a certain breadth is almost inevitable in the framing of the chapters, where larger causes can form a perspective from which we can see smaller events. "As to any provincial history," ends Chapter 35, "in which the agents are all of high moral rank, that must be of a date long posterior to the first Reform Bill, and Peter Featherstone, you perceive, was dead and buried some months before Lord Grey came into office." In *Tom Jones*, setting the fictive events against the historical events of "the '45" is simply a way of authenticating the background of the novel. In *Middlemarch*, to locate the events of the novel in reference to the Reform Bill is to attribute a complex of causes against which the substance of the chapter reverberates.

"More than any of Dickens' previous novels," wrote Steven Marcus,

Dombey and Son directs its attention to the important changes that take place in human life—to birth, marriage and death, to separations and reconciliations, to shipwrecks and bankruptcies. Developing one of the themes of Martin Chuzzlewit, it regards the course of human life in terms of circumstance, of events, forces and laws which are beyond the control of the individual person and indifferent to him. And it is concerned not only with the grand inevitabilities of human experience, but with the kind of compromise and reconciliation they require. In short, it is concerned with blunt necessity and mute submission.[6]

Marcus was speaking of Dickens' thematic concerns, but he might just as easily have been speaking about the organization and segmentation of many Victorian novels. All of the shipwrecks and bankruptcies, the recognitions and leave-takings of Victorian fiction are not only expressions of theme but are also the way in which the structure of a novel is given its substance and the means by which the form of one chapter is given a clarity of outline and a dramatic distinctness from the form of another.

Not only Dickens but novelists as different from each other as Reade and Gissing cause the melodramatic chapter to rise out of convictions and anxieties about the life of their culture. It is not easy to say precisely what separates the brutalities of Smollett's world or the disastrous ineptitudes of Goldsmith's from the accidents and early deaths of the Victorians. In both eighteenth- and nineteenth-century novelists, the blows of circumstance are organized into the major units of the fiction. But it is not too much to say that fortune and misfortune in nineteenth-century chapters is presented so

---

[6] Dickens: From Pickwick to Dombey (New York: Basic Books, 1965), pp. 313–14.

as to be deeply felt by both characters and readers in a way that rarely happens in eighteenth-century fiction and that these events in nineteenth-century fiction are presented so as to suggest largeness of scope, so as to justify the words *laws* and *forces* as Marcus uses them above.

Much of what happens to Dr. Primrose in Goldsmith's *Vicar of Wakefield* might be transferred to any number of Victorian novels, but nothing that happens to Dr. Primrose is the result of laws and forces. To organize a chapter around a personal disaster is hardly an innovation in the nineteenth century, but to invest such a unit with the scope that implies a sort of cultural anxiety *is* a special quality of the nineteenth century, and it carries with it implications involving the tone, the thematic density, and the structural technique of units in Victorian fiction.

A full account of the relation between culture and chapter would have to show the relation between chapters and the substantial development of autobiographical fiction in the nineteenth century; it would have to show the relevance to chapter techniques of such specialized innovations as those of Wilkie Collins in the management of concealment and suspense; and it would have to explore the way in which the personal values of love and loyalty provide the impetus, the vitality, and the resolution to chapters in contrast to the more social values of the eighteenth century. In general, however, and with the heavy qualification that tendencies are being described here, chapters in the nineteenth-century novel represent the segmentation of process, the organization of causal multiplicity, and the objectification of the anxieties of a culture full of stress, human waste, division, and agonizing compromises.

One of the significant developments of fiction in the twentieth century might well have been the disappearance of the chapter. There are probably more reasons why the chapter should have disappeared than reasons why it should have survived. Arnold Hauser, describing the time sense of the twentieth century, wrote of the "amalgamation of space and time," the special value of simultaneity, "the fluidity of the boundaries of space and time," and the way in which cinematic form, more than any other, expresses this time sense. "It is the discontinuity of the plot, the sudden emergence of the thoughts and moods, the relativity and inconsistency of the time-standards, in other words, the effects that remind us of the cuttings, dissolves, and interpolations of the film, which the novels of Proust, Joyce, Dos Passos, and Virginia Woolf have in common." [7]

To Hauser's list of novelists, one might add such names as Faulkner, Gide, and Hesse; and even those novelists who may not seem, in the context of the twentieth century, particularly innovative—Waugh, Henry Green, or Joyce Cary—still project many of the discontinuities that Hauser cites. So many of the techniques of the chapter are so suited to the classic view of time as a uniform flow in a purposeful and intelligible direction that what is remarkable is that the conventions of the chapter have managed to survive at all the breakdown of that view. Yet chapters, however much they may seem to imply the ordered and the soberly sequential, have become a significant means by which a disordered and discontinuous sense of time is expressed.

Since its inception, the "new" novel in France has been belligerently attacked and aggressively defended. Probably no art form since the plays of George Bernard Shaw has been accompanied by so much talk. The movement is certainly less monolithic in theory and practice than it seems from the

[7] "The Conceptions of Time in Modern Art and Science," *Partisan Review*, XXIII (1956), 330–31.

epithet *nouveau roman,* but in its major manifestoes its practitioners present the esthetic values of their work as being contrary to the values traditionally associated with the categories of "character," "story," and "content." [8] Those three categories are traditionally associated with the esthetic possibilities of chaptered narration, and very little in the theory of the new novelists implies the necessity for units, intelligible as units. Yet one picks up a novel by Robbe Grillet, Butor, or Nathalie Sarraute to find it divided. One of the units of Robbe-Grillet's *In the Labyrinth* ends in this way:

An arm remains half raised, a mouth gapes, a head is tipped back; but tension has replaced movement, the features are contorted, the limbs stiffened, the smile has become a grimace, the impulse has lost its intention and its meaning. There no longer remains, in their place, anything but excess, and strangeness, and death. [9]

How successfully the unit that ends at this point actually subverts "character," "story," and "content" is an open question. One aspect of the traditional novel which it does not subvert, however, is the conventions of the chapter. For in its tone, its syntax, its rhythm, its summary, and its philosophical frame, Robbe-Grillet's chapter is made to seem to end in a way that would hardly seem unfamiliar to a reader trained on Victorian novels.

Not only in the "new" novel but elsewhere in twentieth-century fiction subject matter or theme have undergone changes in valuation which undermine the classic validity of the chapter. The word *theme* is an imprecise and elusive one, and different critics will respond to it in different ways. But

---

[8] See, for example, Alain Robbe-Grillet, "Reflections on Some Aspects of the Traditional Novel," *International Literary Annual,* I (1958), 114–21.

[9] *Two Novels by Robbe-Grillet: Jealousy and In the Labyrinth,* trans. Richard Howard (New York: Grove Press, 1965), p. 202.

if one asks how a given chapter of *Bleak House* extends and
develops a theme, the question is reasonable and the answer
accessible. If a chapter written by Samuel Beckett, on the
other hand, extends and develops a theme, its theme can
only be the impossibility of theme. " 'Yes or no?' " asks
Murphy. And Beckett added, "The eternal tautology." In a
world in which *yes* and *no* are tautological, concepts which
lead us to look at a chapter as a self-enclosed block of subject
matter or a stage of thematic development are useless.

In his novel *End of the Road*, John Barth titled each chapter with the first few words from the text of the chapter itself.
Thus, Chapter 4 begins: "I got up, stiff from sleeping in the
chair, showered, changed my clothes, and went out for breakfast." The title of the chapter is "I Got Up, Stiff from Sleeping in the Chair." It is a slight mannerism, odd and amusing,
but in its own way a little shocking. What Barth's title implies is that Chapter 4 is not simply "Chapter 4," which
would be to designate it abstractly as the fourth block of a
developmental whole; it is not "At Wicomico" or "Two
Difficult Days" or "A New Job and an Intriguing Friendship," which would be to locate the chapter spatially, temporally, or substantively; it is not even a block of material,
untitled, separated by white space, which would be to reserve
designation altogether. The implication of Barth's title is
that to state the theme or the subject of the chapter would
be to repeat the words of the chapter, since the chapter has
in no sense of the word a theme, no subject, and is about
nothing which can be abstracted from the totality of the
words on the page. Such a stance is a bit deceptive, of course.
A determined critic with a fondness for thematic analysis
could find *End of the Road* bristling with themes, and the
chapters of the novel do have a unity and coherence enabling
them to be summarized. But one has the sense of perform-

ing these conventional critical acts against the will and contrary to the spirit of Barth. What is remarkable, however, is not that Barth or Beckett should have undercut the possibility of seeing a chapter as an extension of a theme but that the chapter should have survived at all, which, of course, it has.

It is hardly necessary to document, in a book of this scope, the breakdown of reason, order, and unified sensibility in the twentieth century, in public life, in our philosophical assumptions about ourselves, and in our art. Dostoevsky's Underground Man, for whom consciousness is illness and order is aberration, can stand for dozens of philosophical assessments of the modern mind, from Kierkegaard to Jaspers to last week's polemic. There is no philosophical reason why the Underground Man, as speaker of Dostoevsky's novella, should order his reflections into clearly segmented units since everything that seems to justify the chapter is to him an elaborate deception. Yet *Notes from Underground* is made into chapters.

Despite her preoccupation with temporal flux and temporal relativity, Virginia Woolf's novels are made into chapters, or if not chapters, into separated and separable blocks of narrative. Despite his fidelity to the symbology of a dreamlike inner life, Kafka's novels are divided into chapters. Despite its projection of cosmic absurdity, *The Stranger*, by Camus, is divided into chapters and the chapters divided into sections as balanced, as poised and symmetrical as any in prose fiction. Despite the instinctual vitalism and the anti-intellectualism of Lawrence, his novels are made into chapters. Despite its projection of dream, its intricate synthesis of time, history, myth, and language, *Finnegans Wake* is divided into seventeen distinct and explicable chapters. One can cite twentieth-century exceptions: *The Unnamable*, by

Beckett, and *The Leavetaking*, by Peter Weiss, for example. But the fact that both are small novels, novellas really, makes the absence of division less audacious than it would be in a longer work.

The fact is that, whatever the intellectual underpinnings of fiction, the one thing that cannot be avoided, or can be avoided only at considerable peril, is the problem of communication and the realities of perception. That is, one cannot begin to project chaos without the use of order. One cannot demonstrate absurdity without the use of reason. No one really believes that English syntax provides an infallible medium for discussing the world as it is, but one cannot even begin to demonstrate the extent to which we are victimized by syntax without the use of syntax. So it is in fiction. Those conventions of segmentation which have served to cut up so many different kinds of fictional unities cannot easily be dispensed with, even if the classical fictional unities are no longer valid, because one of the important perceptual means by which we understand fiction is narrative division—the chapter.